Emma

The Work, Life, and Style of Emma Stone

Emma

Stacia Deutsch

EPIC INK

Previous: Emma at the 77th Annual Cannes Film Festival, Cannes, France, May 18, 2024

Emma on the red carpet in Cannes, France, May 17, 2024

Contents

INTRODUCTION: The Rise of Emma Stone 7

CHAPTER 1: Setting the Stage 13

CHAPTER 2: Breakout and Breakthrough 27

CHAPTER 3: The Teen Comedy Queen Explores New Horizons 53

CHAPTER 4: Dramatic Depths 81

CHAPTER 5: Balancing Career, Family, and Friendships 109

CHAPTER 6: Cementing Critical Acclaim 131

CHAPTER 7: Emma's Fashion 145

CHAPTER 8: Impact, Influence, and Legacy 167

CONCLUSION: The Next Chapter 183

Filmography 189

Select Awards and Nominations 193

Sources 197

Photo Credits 200

Acknowledgments 203

About the Author 205

Introduction

The Rise of Emma Stone

> "You're only human. You live once and life is wonderful,
> so eat the damn red velvet cupcake."
>
> —Emma in *Glamour*

Emma Stone is used to seeing her name in the news. She's been on the cover of *Vanity Fair*, *Vogue*, *Entertainment Weekly*, and in 2017, was named one of the 100 Most Influential People in the World by *TIME*. Emma's film successes have garnered attention since her breakout in *Easy A* (2010), through *The Help* (2011), *The Amazing Spider-Man* (2012), *Birdman* (2014), and on to her multi-award-winning performance in 2016's *La La Land*. That role, which required the triple threat of acting, singing, and dancing, earned Emma a Best Actress Oscar, among others. After being nominated for another Oscar (for Best Supporting Actress) for 2018's *The Favourite*, Emma continued to shine in role after role. In 2024, she reclaimed the Academy Award spotlight, once again winning Best Actress for *Poor Things*.

While Emma collects milestones such as the highest-paid actress of 2017 and the youngest person to ever host *Saturday Night Live* five times, her philanthropic work leaves the greatest impression. Emma has given her money, time, and energy to boost awareness in the areas of mental health, the environment, gender equality, and, since her mother's own diagnosis and treatment, cancer charities.

Emma at the Chinese Theater in Hollywood, California, for a *La La Land* Press Conference, December 2017

So, it was no surprise when Emma Stone made headlines again in the spring of 2024. But it was not because she'd received another acting award, met a career goal, or paved a new charitable inroad. This time, reporters circled the actor because Emma Stone officially announced that she'd like to be called by a different name.

During an interview with the *Hollywood Reporter*, Nathan Fielder, Emma's costar in the series *The Curse*, told the reporter, "Her name's Emily, but she goes by Emma professionally. So, when there's people that don't know her, I end up saying Emma. But I'm going to just say 'Emily' from here on."

In 2004, Emily Stone chose the name "Emma" because the name "Emily Stone" was already taken by another actor. The actors' union, SAG-AFTRA, discourages two actors from having the same name (to avoid confusion), so if an actor's name is already registered, they'll suggest the applicant take an alternative. Renaming herself wasn't easy, but after some consideration and a few false starts, she looked to Emma Bunton, a member of the British pop group the Spice Girls for inspiration. They were both very blonde, and Emma loved the group; those were reasons enough for young Emily to make the choice. Emily officially became Emma and, from there, "Emma Stone" was an officially registered SAG actor pursuing her Hollywood dreams.

Emma's reaction to Fielder's revelation in the interview was simple. At first, she demurred and told the reporter that she was okay with either name. "You can say Emma. You can say anything." Then she explained further, "I freaked out a couple of years ago. For some reason, I was like, 'I can't do it anymore. Just call me Emily.'"

The *Hollywood Reporter* interview will stand as a turning point in the actor's biography. It marks her transition from child actor, first entering the business through a reality TV competition, to adult, versatile, accomplished star with awards, accolades, and the ability to spearhead dream projects . . . and to reclaim her own name.

Following: Emma attends the 62nd BFI London Film Festival in London, England, October 2018

A Posh Baby

Emma Stone adopted the name "Emma" after Emma Lee Bunton, perhaps better known as Baby Spice of the Spice Girls. Emily. Emma Lee. Emma. It seemed a natural progression.

In fact, back in second grade, Emily had asked her teacher to call her "Emma" after the singer. At the time, the teacher refused. But years later when Emily *had* to choose a name for herself, it was clear that "Emma" was the right fit. But was it *really*?

During an interview with Jimmy Fallon in November 2018, the talk show host led Emma through a *BuzzFeed* quiz called, "Which Spice Girl Are You?" With the very first question, Emma showed the side of her that loves the English language—she even considers herself a grammarian. The question asked her to choose a word from a list of six possibilities and her immediate reply was to point at the first option and gasp, "Loofa? That's supposed to have an h on the end." She didn't pick the misspelled sponge, going for the silly selection of "Dingus" instead.

In a question about hairstyles, she chose "However I woke up," which brought on giggles as Emma revealed that she's really "super low-key." Jimmy didn't buy it, but they moved on.

For the final question, Emma was asked for her favorite Spice Girls song. It was an easy answer, since she'd seen the group multiple times in concert: "I'm going to pick 'Stop,' because 'Stop' is an incredible song."

To Emma's enormous surprise, the quiz revealed that she was *not*, in fact, Emma Bunton, aka Baby Spice. Instead, her replies led to another answer: the English fashion designer and singer Victoria Beckham, aka Posh Spice.

"I'm Posh Spice? That is not—" Emma stammered. "I'm shocked! I'm shocked! I'm shocked!"

"If you live your life on a film set, how the hell can you relate to real people?"

chapter 1

Setting the Stage

"I think my ultimate goal at the end of the day is to make my parents laugh. Maybe that is what this is all about: a roundabout way of trying of trying to entertain my parents, just like I did in the living room when I was a kid."

—Emma in *Glamour*

Emily Jean Stone, the future star who would one day be known the world over as "Emma" Stone, was born in Scottsdale, Arizona, on November 6, 1988. It was a year filled with competition and the seeds of great change. The Winter Olympic Games took place that year in Calgary, Alberta, Canada, with the Summer Games following in Seoul, South Korea, an event that marked South Korea's entry onto the international stage as a global economic partner. George H. W. Bush defeated Michael Dukakis in the US presidential election. The Soviet Union withdrew troops from Afghanistan. Terrorists shot down an airliner over Lockerbie, Scotland.

Emma at the Replay Brand launch party at the Falcon Club in Los Angeles, California, April 2004

Michael Jackson, Bruce Springsteen, Dolly Parton, Milli Vanilli, and Jim Henson were just a few of the celebrities who entertained both on stage and on TV screens at home. Tom Cruise and Bette Midler lit up movie theater marquees as the highest-grossing stars of the year. (Steve Guttenberg took the third spot.) Cruise's *Rain Man* earned four Academy Awards, including Best Picture. While arcades were still popular places for video gaming, the Nintendo Famicom gaming system let users battle it out in *Super Mario Bros.* and *Duck Hunt* at home. Personal computing was in its infancy, though the internet had laid a foundation for future communication, and cell phones, though large and clunky, were finding eager consumers.

Emily Stone entered the world on the cusp of a technological revolution that would touch every aspect of life and make her dreams possible. Due to advances in computing and web access, high school would become more flexible so she could take classes online, opening up precious time to pursue acting. She'd use a popular presentation software program to convince her parents to take her to Hollywood. The world of entertainment stretched out in infinite directions with unlimited possibilities, and the eventual rise of social media would give the actor a massive following, even if she chose not to maintain her own footprint.

Emma was born in Scottsdale, but following her dreams meant a lot of sacrifice. Luckily, her parents and extended family were supportive when she left Arizona, gave up formal education, changed her name, and pursued an acting career.

Her father, Jeffrey Charles Stone, was the CEO and founder of a general contracting company, and her mother, Krista Jean Stone (née Yeager), was a homemaker. Her brother, Spencer, was born two years after Emily. In 2004, she told *People*, "My little brother is my favorite person that's ever lived of all time. I love him so much."

While his sister's star was rising, Spencer reflected on their childhood in an interview with the *Arizona Republic* in 2017. "When I was little, we did our own little shows, and she was the director and

"I wasn't really a tomboy, but I was loud. And bossy. I wanted to be Steve Martin."

bossed me around tremendously, and she would be the star of the show, and I would be everyone else."

Spencer and Emma didn't just create shows, they watched them together too. Comedy was always first choice. During an interview with *W Magazine* in 2011, Emma revealed that the family favorite was Steve Martin's 1979 classic, *The Jerk*. She recalled, "I wasn't really a tomboy, but I was loud. And bossy. I wanted to be Steve Martin."

When Emma was twelve, the family moved onto the property of the Camelback Golf Club and lived on the sixteenth hole. In a 2015 interview with Diane Keaton for *Interview Magazine*, she joked, "It once said on Wikipedia that my parents owned the golf course, which could not be further from the truth. But if you're in Arizona, you're at least within a couple miles of, if not on, a golf course."

Golf was never her thing. Then again, neither was Arizona.

In that same interview, Emma remarked, "I struggle with the desert. Having grown up in Arizona, I struggle with the dryness. I love the heat, but I don't like the dryness . . . And now humidity and heat, oh God, I love it." While young Emma could admit that the sunsets in Arizona were beautiful, and perhaps as an adult she'd give the state another chance, at the time, she knew in her heart that someday she'd have to leave.

When she was seven, Emma was cast in a school play, Carol B. Kaplan's *No Turkey for Perky*. The roles were reserved for fifth grade students, except the part of Perky, the family dog that *really* wants turkey on Thanksgiving. In an interview with *Backstage* in 2024, Emma

> "For a performer at heart, to hear that audience reaction — them laughing? The laughing was like heaven to me."

said, "My teacher, I think, suggested me because I was so loud. For a performer at heart, to hear that audience reaction—them laughing? The laughing was like heaven to me."

At the age of eight, Emma began to suffer from panic attacks. In 2012, she reflected to *ABC News*, "I didn't want to go to my friends' houses or hang out with anybody, and nobody really understood." After a few years of feeling isolated and alone, therapy helped Emma find ways to cope.

Reflecting on her time in the school play and the feeling it gave her, Emma realized that she wanted to recapture that moment in time. Onstage was where she felt good, calm, and focused. She decided to pursue theater.

At the age of eleven, Emma auditioned at Phoenix's Valley Youth Theater. Her first show was *The Wind in the Willows,* and from that moment on, acting truly became her passion. Show after show, she built her skills, expanding into singing and dancing for musical performances. Between the age of eleven and into middle school, Emma was cast in a range of productions including *Titanic*, *Alice in Wonderland*, *The Princess and the Pea*, *Cinderella*, and *The Wiz.*

Bob Cooper, the theater's artistic director, was asked by *Teen Vogue* about Emma's early years in his playhouse. He said, "I knew from a very young age that Emma had the innate ability to bring any character to life. She gives everything to each character she plays and brings truth to the story. Emma knows how to make moments magical."

Cooper explained to ABC 15, "No matter what part she ever got, she would take the role. She didn't have to have the lead. In fact, she never had the lead at Valley Youth Theatre in the 18 shows that she did here."

She also performed with the theater's improvisational comedy troupe. In an interview with *Silve.com* in 2011, Emma spoke about improv comedy and how it directly affected her anxiety. She said, "And that [improv] changed my anxiety forever. Forever. You know how sports teach kids teamwork, and how to be strong and brave and confident? Improv was my sport. I learned how to not waffle and how to

SETTING THE STAGE

"You know how sports teach kids **teamwork,** and how to be **strong** and **brave** and **confident?** **Improv** was my **sport."**

hold a conversation, how to take risks and actually be excited to fail. It taught me so much and helped me overcome so much. And I realized, OK, this is my job."

PROJECT HOLLYWOOD

After one semester at the local all-girl Catholic high school, Emma could see that school wouldn't offer the opportunities that she envisioned for herself. Although she was in one high school play, *Noises Off*, she knew she needed to make a move if she was going to become an actor. Emma immediately began "Project Hollywood," a campaign to convince her family to take her to Los Angeles where she could actively pursue an acting career. She created a PowerPoint presentation and called a family meeting. Recalling the event, she later told *BlackBook*, "It was so silly. I was like fourteen. I used the Madonna song 'Hollywood.' It was ridiculous, like, I used alliteration." But the presentation worked.

Sort of.

Two years earlier, her parents had taken her to Los Angeles for an audition for Nickelodeon's *All That*, a kid's comedy sketch show that would launch Kenan Thompson, Amanda Bynes, and Nick Cannon to stardom. Billed as *Saturday Night Live* for kids, the premise was perfect for Emma. Recalling that experience on *The Tonight Show with Jimmy Fallon* in 2016, Emma admitted she wasn't prepared. "I thought they were going to give us sketches. And then five minutes before I went in the room they said, 'You need to have three characters when you come in the room,'" she explained to Jimmy. "So, I was like, 'Okay,' and then I made up a couple of characters."

Her characters included a cheerleader who couldn't spell and a possessed babysitter, but it wasn't enough to ace the audition. She returned to Arizona and went back to school.

Project Hollywood gave her the second chance she needed, but this time her mom refused to move unless Emma had an agent—no small task for a teenager who wasn't in Los Angeles. While she pondered the problem, her parents thankfully supported her dreams—just closer to home. They had the financial resources to send her to an acting coach in Phoenix who had once worked in Hollywood. In 2011, Emma told *Vanity Fair*, "She [the acting coach] was really helpful because I had been in theater, and she taught me to bring it down in teaspoons instead of buckets because, if you can imagine, I'm really hammy at heart."

In that same *Vanity Fair* interview, she explained, "I have some of the coolest parents in the world. My dad's whole philosophy, my mom's, too, is start with the reins out, and if you do something that should break the trust, then the reins come in—instead of starting the reins in and letting them out—which is awful because it turned me into Pinocchio. That's the only thing that bugged me about it—I can't lie. It really is incredibly hard for me to lie."

Emma recounted an inspirational story to the interviewers, who retold it this way: "When she was thirteen and her friends came to her house at 2 a.m. asking her to sneak out with them, she ran into her mother's bedroom, woke her up, said, 'So-and-so and I are going to sneak out and go to Walmart for Jujubes,' and her mother told her, 'Okay. Take my cell phone, and if you're gone more than an hour, find a way to call me and just say how much longer you'll be.' Emma said, 'They had no idea I told my mom. Since everything was allowed, it made me not want to do crazy shit.'"

All her "hammy" comedy experience paid off when she was granted an audition with an agent in Los Angeles. Using the "I love Josh" monologue from *Clueless*, she wowed the agent at the Savage Agency, a respected talent agency known for placing actors in reputable jobs.

Emma told *Vanity Fair* that she also performed a dramatic monologue that day but couldn't remember what it was—it was comedy that set her on her path. As for the Savage Agency, they were in the right space to get behind her. "Their claim to fame was a bunch of child stars of the day like Rider Strong and Ben Savage—basically the whole cast of *Boy Meets World*," she explained. Once the papers were signed,

Emma had done exactly what her parents requested: she'd found herself representation. As she told the *Hollywood Reporter* in 2017, "It's nuts that they [her parents] agreed to it. I don't condone it. Everybody should go through high school and graduate."

And so, in 2004, when she was only fifteen years old, Emma's mother moved with her to Los Angeles, while her brother and father remained in Phoenix. Her mom rented an apartment for six months; in that time, they'd know if they'd made the right decision or not. Going home was always an option.

EMMA VERSUS THE OAKWOOD

According to the 2011 *Vanity Fair* interview, at the time of Emma's big move, there was an apartment complex in LA that was rife with young actors. The Oakwood Apartments was a vast compound of a thousand apartments catering to parents with children trying to break into Hollywood. Budding stars like Miley Cyrus, Hilary Duff, Keshia Knight Pulliam, and Frankie Muniz all lived at the complex for a while when they were starting out. Producers, aspiring directors, and even Jay Leno were said to roam the halls looking for talent. The apartment also boasted an activities department that focused on helping up-and-comers navigate the industry.

Emma's mom made a strategic decision to steer clear of Oakwood and the hub of competition there. Instead, she rented a place in Park La Brea, a sprawling community that attracted a more settled LA population.

Every day, Emma would face the actors from Oakwood. It was a time of huge growth for Disney shows, all of which required young players. In 2004, the network launched *Dave the Barbarian* and *Phil of the Future*, while continuing successful shows like *That's So Raven* and *Lizzie McGuire*, and movies such as *Halloweentown High*. *The Suite Life of Zack and Cody* launched the following year. *High School Musical* and *Hannah Montana* were in the works, prepping for success as well.

SETTING THE STAGE 21

Nickelodeon was also rolling out premier content, with *Drake & Josh* and *Ned's Declassified School Survival Guide* as their 2004 hits.

Emma auditioned for any show that fit her skills. Unfortunately, rejection notices often followed, one after the other. She filled her time with online high school courses and a part-time job at a bakery that made cookies for dogs.

In 2024, she told *Backstage* that she was spurred by the feeling that, "If I don't get to act, I will die." With that emotional drive, Emma threw herself into her craft. She brought her comedic energy to auditions and leaned into her naturally raspy voice as an acting tool. "I had colic from zero to six months. I screamed myself hoarse every day, and developed nodules as an infant," she said in an interview with *Now Toronto*. While Emma often struggled with voice loss after long rehearsals, her voice also made her distinct. Since there wasn't anything she could do about the way she sounded, she quickly found that leaning into the rasp set her apart from other actors. Emma admitted to Biogragphy.com in 2024 that she also dyed her naturally blonde hair brown in hopes that it would make her look like a more serious actor. She would have taken any role, any genre, but none were offered.

While talking to Vinnie Mancuso at *Backstage*, Emma focused on the way that desperation drove her during those days. "Which is how I think you do know you're an actor: when it feels so dramatic, the idea that you wouldn't get to do it," she reflected. "It really solidifies the pain that you're in—[which,] as an actor, is worth it."

Finally, a door opened.

Actually, it was her mom who opened it.

In the 2011 *Vanity Fair* interview, Emma explained that her mom saw an ad on TV for a VH1 reality show called *In Search of the New Partridge Family*. The plan was to then launch a scripted series with the winning cast of the reality show. Much like the original *The Partridge Family* from the 1970s, the comedy would follow the ups and downs of creating a family band. The show was going to be stylized with direct to camera interviews, much like the 2009 *Modern Family*, in a mockumentary style.

Her mom saw the advertisement, turned, and nodded towards Emma's brown hair. She said, "You look like Susan Dey—maybe you could be a Partridge."

Auditions required both singing and acting talent. Though Emma didn't see herself as a competent singer, she'd sang and danced in musical theater in Arizona and excelled at musical performances. In an interview with *Vogue* in 2014, she said, "You go in there rolling your eyes, thinking, 'this is just a reality search competition,' but then you're there for seven weeks, and you just really, really want to win."

During the competition, she belted out "We Belong" by Pat Benatar and Meredith Brooks' song "Bitch." Emma wowed the judges. Luckily, she also looked enough like the original Laurie Partridge to clinch the win. Her name, still Emily Stone at the time, would be in the credits of a real Hollywood production. There was no need to move back to Arizona—she was going to be a TV star.

"You go in there rolling your eyes, thinking, 'This is just a reality search competition,' but then you're there for seven weeks, and you just really, really want to win."

SETTING THE STAGE

Emma's First Job in Hollywood

After moving to Hollywood with her mom, Emma knew she needed a job, something to give her a little income while auditioning. It had to have flexible hours that would also allow her to call out whenever there was a casting opportunity. She was only fifteen, so what could she do?

Emma and her mom lived across the street from the historic Farmers' Market near The Grove, an iconic shopping mall. There, at the Three Dog Bakery, she found a gig: baking cookies for dogs. In August 2011, she told *Vanity Fair*, "I think three people called my specific cookies inedible to their dogs. I'm not a super-talented dog baker."

This early beginning has turned into a legendary story for the actor. In 2016, she gave some extra details about her role at the bakery, recounting to *Vogue* some of the better recipes in her repertoire. "Pup Tarts. Pop Tarts, but for dogs. And Pupcakes," she explained. "Then there was a kind of dog Oreo made with carob and honey. A mom would come in and buy them for her kid because she thought dog Oreos were healthier."

In a goofy TikTok moment with her friend; actor Jennifer Lawrence, Emma mentioned that her first job was at a dog bakery. Jennifer, faux-horrified replied, "You baked dogs?!" To which Emma, without missing a beat, displayed her finely tuned acting skills. She turned and gave Jennifer a sincere, apologetic glance, then responded, "Yeah. We'll talk about it later . . ."

Thankfully—for both Emma and the local dog population—Emma didn't need to bake dog cookies for long. A few months into her new Hollywood life, she began to land small roles and regular acting work.

chapter 2

Breakout
and
Breakthrough

"Nobody knows what they're doing! We're all just a bunch of
people trying to figure out how to get through the day."

—Emma interviewed for a *British Vogue* cover story in 2018

Spencer Tuskowski was Emma's costar on *The New Partridge Family*.
In a Reddit comment, he talked about the show: "It was written by
two old writers from *The Simpsons*. At the time [the reality show] got
actually pretty good viewership. The pilot was ahead of its time though
and people didn't understand that it was built as though we were a *real*
singing family and VH1 was 'following us around.' It's a shame because
just a few years later, you get *Modern Family*, and everybody loves
that show. I think they tried to do too much away from the original
sitcom that everyone loved, unfortunately. We shot this episode [the
pilot in the video on Reddit] for a week, and honestly some of the best
memories I'll have for the rest of my life."

Emma on the red carpet for the premiere of *Poor Things* at the Barbican Centre in London, England, December 2023

In the video's comments, Spencer also shed a little light on the audition process for the show through *In Search of the New Partridge Family.*

"Each character had eight people vying for the role, and we slowly got eliminated down to one for each," he explained. "It was such a fun time and honestly thought I'd be famous from it! (Was thirteen and naive lol). It's cool to see Emily blew up though!"

During an interview with writer Luke Crisell, Emma added her own comment about the audition process. "It was an open call, like *American Idol.* I had a number pinned to my chest." She went on to say, "But it was the one time my mom has ever pushed me to do anything. She kept saying, 'I have this weird gut feeling.'"

Her mom's "gut feeling" paid off and Spencer was right: Emma certainly did "blow up" after this first step into Hollywood. Though the scripted show was canceled after the pilot, the experience landed her a relationship with Doug Wald, a manager.

As Emma told Crisell of Doug Wald, "He's the professional love of my life. He talks me through everything."

Starring in *The New Partridge Family* brought increased interest in Emma, and with Doug's help, she began auditioning for new roles on television. It was 2005, and Emma was on her way to becoming a professional actor in Hollywood, meaning it was time to join the Screen Actors Guild-American Federation of Television and Radio Artists, SAG-AFTRA, the labor union that represents media artists. She applied under her own name, Emily Stone, and it was a big surprise to find out that her name was already registered to another actor! To avoid confusion, SAG-AFTRA doesn't allow two actors to perform under the same name, and Emily Stone was a contestant on Australia's Next Top Model.

Emma would need another name.

As Emma told *W Magazine* in 2017, "To ask a sixteen-year-old to pick a new name is a really interesting process." What would the directors call her? Which name would go in the show credits? Emma didn't know what to do. SAG offered her Emily J. Stone, adding the initial for her middle name (Jean), but she didn't want her name to sound like a take-off of Michael J. Fox's name. In a video of that same *W* interview, she giggles, "I didn't think I could pull off the J."

> "To ask a sixteen-year-old to pick a new name is a really interesting process."

Emma was cast for one episode on the show *Medium*, which aired in 2005. The next year, she appeared on one episode on the *Suite Life of Zack and Cody* as the voice of a dog, Ivana Tipton. As she told *W*, the pressure was on to pick a name. "I was like, 'I'm going to be Riley. My name is going to be Riley Stone.'"

"Riley" appeared in the credits for *Medium* in 2005. But when another show came her way, Emma began to have doubts.

She admitted to *W*, "I did a guest spot on *Malcolm in the Middle*, and one day they were like, 'Riley! Riley!' and I had no idea who they were talking to. They were like 'Hey, hey, come on. We need you on set.' And I was like, 'Oh, I'm not Riley. I can't be Riley.'"

Emma returned to the SAG offices, with new inspiration in mind: a Spice Girl. She looked to Emily "Emma" Bunton, aka. Baby Spice, and, as she explained on *The Tonight Show with Jimmy Fallon* in 2018, "So growing up I was super blonde, and my real name is Emily, but I wanted to be called Emma because of Baby Spice and guess what, now I am." Most of her friends and colleagues found a compromise and call her "Em" while those who know her well call her "Emily" when they're together.

In 2007, when the newly christened Emma Stone was seventeen, she found regular work on a Fox drama called *Drive*, about competitors in an illegal underground cross-country race. The show fell on the heels of her first movie, *Superbad*. She'd already filmed *Superbad*, but it was being edited when she landed the TV gig. *Drive* aired four months before *Superbad* hit theaters.

In *Drive*, her hair was no longer the Emma Bunton-blonde that had partly inspired Emma's name. Emma was a redhead, which would become her signature style. In 2017, *Elle* reported that Judd Apatow, writer and producer of *Superbad*, was the one to suggest the change. In a 2002 interview with *Vanity Fair*, Apatow recalled how he made the beauty suggestion. "There was a concern that [Emma] had the same color hair as Martha MacIsaac's [in *Superbad*]," he told the magazine. "And I said, 'Well, maybe it could be like red or something.' So we dyed her hair red, which I think she had never done before. And since then, she has cursed me because now people love her with red hair, and she's had to live with that for a lot of her adult life."

Emma was more than willing to dye her hair for the role and didn't change it when *Drive* came along. Since Apatow's suggestion, Emma's hair color has become part of her brand and identity. In 2013, she even told *Stylecaster*, "I identify most with red hair. My mom's a redhead, so maybe I grew up seeing it more than seeing myself in a mirror. But I like blonde too. It's just hair."

The stage was set for Emma's new look as she stepped onto the set of *Drive*. In an interview with *IGN*, Emma talked about the process of being in a TV show that depended heavily on visual effects. Since *Drive* was about a cross-country race, some of the scenes were filmed outside, but many took place in a studio against a green screen.

"I identify most with red hair. My mom's a redhead, so maybe I grew up seeing it more than seeing myself in a mirror. But I like blonde too. It's just hair."

"I think it's interesting, the whole being on a green screen all the time," she mused. "When Natalie Portman was in *Star Wars*, she kept talking about . . . how it's like playing in a refrigerator box, which is completely true because you have to completely imagine your surroundings and you're going like a hundred miles an hour. And there's all this crazy stuff going around you, people cutting you off, and you're sitting, literally, in a lime green room."

Drive didn't get the kind of ratings that Fox expected and within a few months, they canceled the series. Six episodes had been filmed, though of those, only four premiered on Fox. The last two were put online, available for streaming only via Fox On Demand in 2007.

While the show didn't get the viewership the network had hoped, it marked an unexpected milestone. In 2007, the show had been considered for an Emmy Award for Outstanding Visual Effects in a Drama Series, but a show needed to air at least six episodes to be eligible for an Emmy. That year, however, the Emmy Awards opened a new category for streaming. Because the last two episodes had been aired online, it became eligible for the award as Outstanding Visual

Emma stars in *Superbad*, 2007.

Effects in a Television Miniseries, Movie, or Special. *Drive* holds a historic place as the first series to be nominated under the new Emmy guidelines.

For Emma, the cancellation of *Drive* was disappointing, but not the worst hit she had taken around that time. Before *Drive* or *Superbad*, she'd auditioned for the role of Claire Bennet in *Heroes*, the science-fiction drama that would go on to air on NBC for four years. As Emma sat waiting outside the audition room, she heard the casting team offer the role to Hayden Panettiere.

"Before I went in, I heard them saying to the girl ahead of me, 'You've got the part. You're the best fit,'" she explained to Red Bull's *Red Bulletin*. "It was Hayden Panettiere. A big part of me died inside right there. I thought, 'I'm just going to get rejected my whole life, and just keep hearing no, no, no.'"

As she remembered to *Vanity Fair*, "I went home and just had this meltdown."

She went on in the *Red Bulletin* interview to say, "Then I got my part in *Superbad* two weeks after that. That changed my life forever. It taught me to make the best out of difficult situations."

Emma has a tattoo to remind her of all her ups and downs. She told the *Red Bulletin* that the tattoo was designed by Paul McCartney. "It's two bird footprints, because my mother's favorite love song is 'Blackbird' by the Beatles, and because of the great line in the song," about learning how to fly.

And fly she did.

A SUPER-*GOOD* OPPORTUNITY

Looking back on *Superbad*, Judd Apatow told Masterclass: "When we met Emma Stone on *Superbad*, we thought, she's a great actress, she's the most likable person I've ever seen, and she also seems smart and funny and the type of person who in high school would like Jonah. She'd be able to see that beneath all of his bluster was a great guy, and

Emma co-starring with actor Jonah Hill in *Superbad*, August, 2007

that made us love her. That's what made their relationship so realistic and sweet and funny. Because two people that seemed very different are actually perfect together."

The movie's director, Greg Mottola, was interviewed in 2017's *Vanity Fair* story about Emma. He said, "There was talk about hiring slightly more conventional fantasy types for these two roles [the love interests for Jonah Hill and Michael Cera]. But I argued that Emma's gorgeous and has a lot of skills. What really struck me was the surprise of the character; you think she's a party girl, but she ends up being far more mature than the other characters in the script—nobody could pull that off like she could."

In 2008, *Superbad* was nominated for five MTV Movie Awards, and Emma Stone won a Young Hollywood Exciting New Face Award for her role. But the big prize for Emma was that *Superbad* brought her together with her best friend Martha MacIsaac. Though Emma spent only eight days on set for filming, the two of them lived together

Emma Stone as Jules in *Superbad*, 2007

Emma Stone, Teddy Geiger, Josh Gad, and Rainn Wilson in *The Rocker*, 2008

Opposite: Emma Stone in *The Rocker*, 2008

BREAKOUT AND BREAKTHROUGH

for years following the *Superbad* shoot. Their friendship continued as they each took on other roles, with social media acting as a record of their trips to wineries, award shows, and more. In 2017, the duo got the chance to act together again in *Battle of the Sexes*, and Martha was a bridesmaid at Emma's 2020 wedding.

After *Superbad*, next up for Emma was a film called *The Rocker*. For this, a 2008 film, Emma needed to learn bass guitar. She played all the songs in the film herself, though not on the soundtrack. She just wanted her movements, as she performed, to look authentic. The movie was about a failed musician who joins his nephew's band, hoping for a comeback. Emma performed with Rainn Wilson, Christina Applegate, and Jason Sudeikis. Teddy Geiger was also in the film, and the two struck up a quiet relationship. Emma and Teddy maintained privacy as the film opened and they embarked on interviews together to promote it.

Although the film got mediocre reviews, Emma, as a comedy actor, was unstoppable.

Emma as Allison Vandermeersh alongside Matthew McConaughey in *Ghosts of Girlfriends Past*, May 2009

"I really enjoyed playing a character outside of the box and hope to continue to do so."

Following *The Rocker* came *The House Bunny*. In that film, Anna Faris played a Playboy Bunny kicked out of the mansion who takes a job as a house mother in a sorority house, and Emma was one of the university students. She originally auditioned for the role of Ashley, the snobby leader of a rival sorority, but was hired instead to play Natalie, a shy character looking to gain more confidence. Emma told *North By Northwestern*, "I got into comedy through improv and sketch comedy. So where in other roles I've been sort of the straight man, it was nice to be able to do that improv and sketch comedy on film and really create Natalie and that whole arc. I really enjoyed playing a character outside of the box and hope to continue to do so."

Her comedy sensibilities propelled her forward and in 2009, Emma was in three films back-to-back: *Ghosts of Girlfriends Past*, *Paper Man*, and *Zombieland*.

Emma with co-stars Jesse Eisenberg, Abigail Breslin, and Woody Harrelson in a scene from the first *Zombieland* movie, October 2009

Ghosts of Girlfriends Past put her on film with Matthew McConaughey and Jennifer Garner. Emma's role was minor but provided another showcase for her humor. *Paper Man* starred Jeff Daniels and Ryan Reynolds. Emma played a teenager who helps Jeff with his character's issues. The film received mixed reviews, but Jeff Daniels and Emma Stone were praised for their work.

Speaking to Backstage.com in 2024, Emma reflected on her relationship to *Zombieland* costar Jesse Eisenberg, saying, "We realized we were maybe the only two people that either of us would ever meet that actually saw *Titanic: The Musical* on Broadway."

Woody Harrelson related a story about Emma when they were in *Zombieland* together. He went to dinner with Emma and her dad while on set. In *Vanity Fair*, Woody recounted, "She's got this kind of completeness to her. I always think of her as a young Lauren Bacall.

An action shot of Emma in the first *Zombieland* movie, October 2009

BREAKOUT AND BREAKTHROUGH

She's got a voice forty years older than she is. When God put the person together, He got the wrong voice."

It wasn't just her voice that stuck with Woody that night. His own daughter was also at the meal, listening intently as Emma talked about Project Hollywood and the PowerPoint presentation that got her to Los Angeles. Woody turned to his daughter and said, "No matter what you do, you're not moving to LA."

By the end of the year, LA wasn't the right place for Emma either. Now that she was getting film and television offers, she no longer needed to be close to Hollywood and the audition process. Emma was in demand. She could travel to a set from anywhere.

In 2009, she moved to New York City. As she told *Vanity Fair*, "I actually like LA a lot more now that I don't live there." In New York, Emma took advantage of the arts, theater, and food scenes. At first, she lived in Greenwich Village, which had an appealing energy and diversity, and she quickly found that she loved walking through neighborhoods, exploring, and taking advantage of the anonymity that New York can offer a busy celebrity.

After returning to her *Zack and Cody* roots by voicing another dog in *Marmaduke*, Emma found her groove, and stardom, in 2010's quirky soon-to-be-classic *Easy A*.

Easy A presents a modern twist on *The Scarlet Letter* by Nathaniel Hawthorne. Olive, a high school student, is judged by her classmates when a (false) story about a tryst with a college guy spreads like wildfire. Inspired by her English class reading, she not only takes on a scarlet letter, but also allows the rumors to propagate, using her new status to aid fellow outsiders. The film takes a deep, and comedic, dive into what it means to live in the shadow of rumors and judgment.

The role was perfect for Emma. After getting the role after an online audition, she also convinced the producers to cast her brother Spencer in a small role. He can be seen as an extra in a party scene.

In an interview with Cinemablend.com, Emma spoke about the video diary scenes, which allow Olive to tell audiences her side of the

40 EMMA

Stanley Tucci and Emma Stone in *Easy A*, 2010

Emma Stone in *Easy A*, 2010

Following: Emma as Olive Penderghast in *Easy A*, September 2010

BREAKOUT AND BREAKTHROUGH

"I remember the day I wrapped *Easy A*. Getting into the car as the sun was coming up because it had been a night shoot … It felt like a house had been lifted off of me."

story in between flashbacks to the events as they unfold. Emma filmed those scenes herself at home, without a crew. "I was not happy, needless to say, when he [director Will Gluck] asked me to do that. It's like a one-minute monologue, and I did it over and over and over." Emma is a perfectionist and choosing the right take was difficult. "Then, finally, my roommate was like, just send it."

In 2018, during *Variety*'s "Actors on Actors," Emma admitted to Timothée Chalamet that *Easy A* wasn't easy for her.

She said, "I was 20 and I put so much pressure on myself. While we were shooting it, I was just going nuts and was like, 'I don't know, this whole thing could fall apart, I have no idea.' Because I had to be there all day, every day. And if I wasn't on screen, I was narrating, and it was

Emma acting in a scene from *Easy A*, September 2010

just too much me." When asked about seeing the film, Emma said, "I haven't seen it. No, I've seen some scenes. But I went to a friends and family screening to see it, and I had to get up and walk out. Who wants to watch themselves for that long?"

To *Far Out Magazine*, Emma expanded on the experience. "I remember the day I wrapped *Easy A*," she said. "Getting into the car as the sun was coming up because it had been a night shoot . . . It felt like a house had been lifted off of me."

Once the movie was released, *Easy A* was a huge hit for Emma. Her rendition of Natasha Bedingfield's "Pocketful of Sunshine," performed over the course of several scenes as Olive spends an uneventful weekend at home, was hugely popular. The movie went on to receive

Aly Michalka (Rhiannon) and Emma (Olive) in *Easy A*, September 2010

BREAKOUT AND BREAKTHROUGH

the Critic's Choice Award for Best Film. For her role as Olive, Emma received a Teen Choice Award and her first nomination for a Golden Globe. In September 2010, famed film critic Roger Ebert wrote, "It's a funny, engaging comedy that takes the familiar but underrated Emma Stone and makes her, I believe, a star." Patricia Clarkson, who played Emma's mom in the film, talked to *The Independent* about meeting Emma on set and called her "a force to be reckoned with from the moment we started shooting."

The film was a major stepping stone for Emma's career, but the film is also now known for being Amanda Bynes's last on-screen performance. Having struggled with body image and mental health, the popular comedic actor left the film industry after *Easy A*. She told *Paper Magazine*, "I literally couldn't stand my appearance in that movie, and I didn't like my performance. I was absolutely convinced I needed to stop acting after seeing it." While drug use contributed to the feeling that she needed to "retire," Amanda Bynes continued to drift.

Discussing her own battles with mental health, Emma told *Rolling Stone* in 2019 that starting therapy as a child helped her find coping mechanisms when her issues first arose. "It [therapy] helped so much. I wrote this book called *I Am Bigger Than My Anxiety* that I still have: I drew a little green monster on my shoulder that speaks to me in my ear and tells me all these things that aren't true. And every time I listen to it, it grows bigger. If I listen to it enough, it crushes me. But if I turn my head and keep doing what I'm doing—let it speak to me, but don't give it the credit it needs—then it shrinks down and fades away."

Easy A was a stressful project, but with help, Emma found her way to the other side. In 2010, she pressed forward. Not only did Emma continue to appear in films and television at breakneck speed, but her face was now plastered on popular magazine covers. After the success of *Easy A*, everyone wanted to know more about Emma Stone.

Taylor Swift, Emma, and Ashley Avignone at the premiere of *Easy A* at the Chinese Theater in Los Angeles, California, September 2010

Following: Emma during the 75th Venice Film Festival for *The Favourite* in Italy, August 2018

"If I listen to it [my anxiety] enough, it crushes me. But if I turn my head and keep doing what I'm doing — let it speak to me, but don't give it the credit it needs — then it shrinks down and fades away."

The Sexy Surprise

During the filming of *Easy A*, there is a scene where Emma pretends to have sex with a guy at a party. The whole thing is fake, with the two of them putting on a show, jumping on the bed while screaming and moaning. But, during the filming, something very real happened to Emma. Suddenly, she struggled to breathe.

Emma had not been diagnosed with asthma before that event. In fact, she thought she was just in poor physical shape. She later told MTV News, "Oh, for the love, I can't even simulate sex without dying! I had a little asthma attack, without any prior knowledge that I had asthma, during the scene where we had to jump up and down for hours and hours screaming and yelling on the bed. [It] was humiliating, because it was the second day of shooting."

In that same 2010 interview, she imagined what must have been going on in the mind of the onset crew: "Here's what it's going to be like the whole movie, as I'm breathing into an oxygen tank. The crew was like, 'She's going to be a real blast. Wow. Amazing. A twenty-year-old having an asthma attack.'"

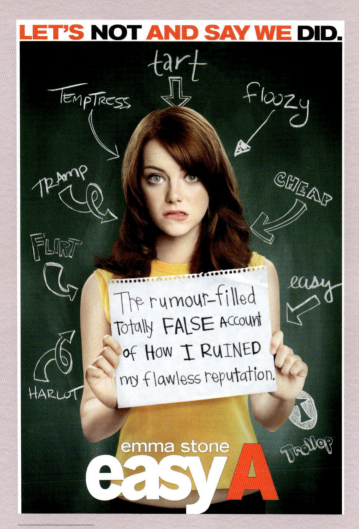

Film poster for *Easy A*, September 2010

The Teen Comedy Queen Explores New Horizons

chapter 3

"In real life, sometimes it's uncomfortable for me not to go for the joke. . . . Often, joking for me is a way of diffusing the awkwardness of a situation, so it's kind of exhilarating to be a part of projects where there's nothing funny or lighthearted."

—Emma interviewed for a *W* cover story in 2013

By 2010, all eyes were on Emma Stone. People especially wanted to know more about her relationship with Teddy Geiger, who she had met when she was first finding her feet in LA at the auditions for *In Search of the Partridge Family*. The two reconnected and started dating while filming *The Rocker*. The relationship lasted nearly two years but ended before Emma's 2009 career explosion. Geiger went into music full time. In 2017, Teddy Geiger revealed to fans that she was transgender, and

---

Emma attending the *Irrational Man* photocall at the 68th Cannes Film Festival in Cannes, France, May 2015

years later, remains one of the most influential openly trans people in music production.

In 2009, while on the set of *Paper Man*, Emma met Keiran Culkin. They played a couple in the movie, which naturally sparked rumors of a real-life relationship. The press buzzed when they were occasionally spotted at events together, but whatever happened between them remained private, and they never revealed the details. In 2024, when talking to *Rolling Stone* about his film *A Real Pain*, produced by Emma, Keiran said, "It's funny to even say 'ex.' To me, she's just a really good friend of mine and my wife's. She's lovely and great."

During the two years when she might, or might not, have been dating Keiran, Emma was cast in a lot of new projects. She voiced

Emma and Ryan Gosling starring in *Crazy, Stupid, Love*, July 2011

Mazie, an Australian shepherd, in the 2010 movie *Marmaduke*. The cast also included superstars like Owen Wilson, Sam Elliott, and William H. Macy. The film wasn't well received, but Emma's next role would propel her further into the spotlight.

Crazy, Stupid, Love was a sleeper comedy that paired Emma with Ryan Gosling. At the time, Ryan wasn't working in comedy, but he wanted to work with Emma, so he signed on. In 2023, *FandomWire* quoted Gosling as saying, "Well, it's tough with Emma because we are such knuckleheads, and we have to work hard to be serious. Especially as we got to know each other on a comedy [*Crazy, Stupid, Love*]."

Filming with Ryan brought out the silliness in them both. During an interview with BBC One, Emma talked about the *Dirty Dancing* lift

Ryan as Jacob and Emma as Hannah in a scene from *Crazy, Stupid, Love*, July 2011

THE TEEN COMEDY QUEEN EXPLORES NEW HORIZONS

they did in the film. She didn't realize until they were on set that she was afraid to be lifted. Looking back, she should have known because as a child, she'd broken both arms when she fell in a gymnastics class.

"I run to do the lift. Ryan lifts me over his head and . . ." She paused and gave the story to Ryan to finish.

"I've never had this happen," he explained, "but I'd imagine if an opossum fell out of a tree and started to scratch your eyes out—it would be something similar."

Emma laughed. "It was a lot. And then, I had a full meltdown."

She crawled into bed and had a cryfest while watching *Labyrinth*. After checking on her, directors Glenn Ficarra and John Requa decided to use a stunt double. Looking back, Emma laughs about the whole thing.

The sense of humor that Emma brings to her projects is contagious and is partly why the same actors end up doing multiple projects with her. Lisa Kudrow joined her in both *Easy A* and *Paper Man*; *Friends with Benefits* brought Emma back onto the screen with Woody Harrelson; and she'd also appear in *Gangster Squad* and *La La Land* with Ryan Gosling.

But before reteaming with Ryan, Emma took on a role that would expand her acting, away from comedy and into drama.

In 2011, she was cast in the drama *The Help*, based on the novel by Kathryn Stockett. The novel and film follow a young white woman, Skeeter Phelan (played in the film by Emma), who grew up in the South and aims to help Black housekeepers unveil the stories of racism and hardship they face.

Emma did not get an award for the movie, but *The Help* was nominated for four Academy Awards, including a nomination for Octavia Spencer for Best Supporting Actress—an award she won. In a 2017 *Vanity Fair* interview, Emma said, "It's really rewarding, and all those adjectives, to do something heartbreaking, but *The Help* is actually really funny—I mean, not incredibly funny, but there are some funny lines."

Co-stars Emma (Eugenia 'Skeeter'), Octavia Spencer (Minny), and Viola Davis (Aibileen) in a scene from *The Help*, August 2011

Emma in *The Help*, August 2011

THE TEEN COMEDY QUEEN EXPLORES NEW HORIZONS

Emma was chosen for one big reason. As the *Vanity Fair* article explains, when searching for his lead, director Tate Taylor asked himself, "Who's got that Joan Cusack quality who's self-deprecating but not a train wreck?" Emma was suggested, but he didn't know her. "I sat down and met her at the Four Seasons, and I said, 'Yes, this is my Joan Cusack,'" he said.

The Help was widely acclaimed, though it also received criticism for portraying a "white savior" narrative. Regarding this criticism, Emma responded in an interview with *Time Out*, "I just do not see Skeeter as a 'savior,' [*gets close to the recorder*] and I'm putting that in quotes. She's idealistic and she really wants to be published, and that's how it begins, not out of martyrdom or being revolutionary. Skeeter just comes up with an idea. Aibileen's brave enough to go through with it."

Emma with *The Help*'s castmates Viola Davis, Octavia Spencer, Allison Janney, and screenwriter Kathryn Stockett at the 37th Deauville American Film Festival in France, September 2011

Each part that Emma chose to take on brought her more and more into the public eye. But there was one thing that she'd kept private during the filming of all those films. Back in 2008, when Emma's star was just beginning to blaze, her mother had been diagnosed with breast cancer. By 2010, her mother was in remission, and Emma revealed the experience on the *Late Show with David Letterman*. She also explained that her blackbird tattoo, designed by Paul McCartney, was in honor of her mother's remission, adding that she and her mother have the same tattoo.

In 2013, *Glamour* reported that Emma said of her mother's cancer diagnosis and battle, "I was oddly stoic, the opposite of how I usually am. But it was terrifying."

With each film's success, Emma's private life, and the lives of her family members, grew harder to protect. Her next film would blow open her dating life.

Emma portraying Eugenia 'Skeeter' Phelan in *The Help*, August 2011

THE TEEN COMEDY QUEEN EXPLORES NEW HORIZONS

Emma (Gwen Stacy) and Andrew Garfield (Peter Parker) in *The Amazing Spider-Man 2*, May 2014

Opposite: Film poster for *The Amazing Spider-Man* starring Emma and Andrew Garfield, July 2012

Following: *The Amazing Spider-Man 2* co-stars, Emma and Andrew Garfield, at the world premiere at The Odeon Leicester Square in London, England, April 2014

AN *AMAZING* RELATIONSHIP

Emma met Andrew Garfield on the set of 2012's *The Amazing Spider-Man*. Andrew played Peter Parker and Emma portrayed Gwen Stacy, a love interest for the web-slinger. Their on-screen chemistry moved out of the film when the two began officially dating after the film's release.

Andrew Garfield talked about his feelings for Emma in an interview that can be found on the special features for *The Amazing Spider-Man*'s Blu-ray/DVD release. He said, "She was like a shot of espresso. She's like being bathed in the sunlight. She's incredibly energetic and enthusiastic and she had this sense of play and fun which was incredibly exciting."

It has been reported that Emma's relationship with Andrew was a dynamic part of filming, bringing added chemistry to the characters. Andrew Garfield continued to gush about Emma in *Teen Vogue*. "She was the last person to screen-test, and I was so bored of it by then that I was mucking about," he said. "And then she came in, and it was like diving into white-water rapids and having no desire to hang on to the side. Throughout shooting, it was wild and exciting. I couldn't help but

"Meeting Andrew, and working with Andrew ... it was one of the greatest experiences I've ever had."

"I'm so lucky that I've gotten to play independent, smart women that are strong and sure of themselves. But there's something about Gwen that is kind of the ultimate damsel in distress, and I was also attracted to that, to that side of women that [says], 'Wait! Save me!'"

try to stay with her, keep pace with her, and not let her get away. Like an animal preying on a smaller animal, but a wily smaller animal."

While Andrew's comments are over the top, Emma gave a similar reply about working with Andrew in that interview. She'd been offered a part in *21 Jump Street* when she went to meet Andrew for *Spider-Man*.

"And then I tested with him, and that sealed the deal," she told *Teen Vogue*. "Because meeting Andrew, and working with Andrew—cover your ears, Andrew, earmuffs—it was one of the greatest experiences I've ever had."

The relationship was magical, but the character drew Emma into the project. She said to Gamesradar.com, "I'm so lucky that I've gotten to play independent, smart women that are strong and sure of themselves. But there's something about Gwen that is kind of the ultimate damsel in distress, and I was also attracted to that, to that side of women that [says], 'Wait! Save me!'" With that, she chose to do her own stunts, insisting it was nothing dangerous or crazy, but allowed her another step into the character.

Emma and Andrew dated for four years, through the filming of *The Amazing Spider-Man 2* and the world tour that followed in 2014. When they were out, the duo often wrote notes for the paparazzi, holding them in front of their faces and directing viewers to charities, like Gilda's Club NYC and Youth Mentoring Connection.

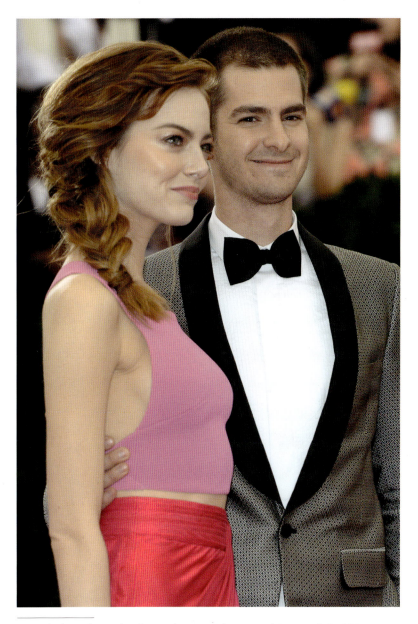

Emma and Andrew at the Met Gala at the Metropolitan Museum of Art in New York City, New York, May 2014

THE TEEN COMEDY QUEEN EXPLORES NEW HORIZONS

A scene from *La La Land* co-starring Ryan Gosling (Sebastian) and Emma (Mia), December 2016

Behind the scenes footage of *Gangster Squad* with Ryan Gosling (Sgt. Jerry Wooters) and Emma (Grace Faraday), January 2013

Opposite: Emma in December 2011 for *The Amazing Spider-Man*

THE TEEN COMEDY QUEEN EXPLORES NEW HORIZONS

In 2015, Emma and Andrew realized they had different long-term goals and separated. But their friendship and love for each other continued. In 2016, Andrew was asked by the *Hollywood Reporter* who he'd take with him on a deserted island. Andrew replied, "Emma Stone. I love Emma. She's all right. She can come." In 2017, there were rumors they were back together after Emma was seen in London at a play that Andrew starred in. A year later, the two were seen having dinner in New York City.

When Andrew returned to the *Spider-Man* franchise for the third film, *Spider-Man: No Way Home*, he kept his cameo a secret. But someone was determined to learn the truth. *People* reported in 2022 that Andrew said, "Emma kept on texting me. She was like, 'Are you in this new *Spider-Man* film?' And I was like, 'I don't know what you're talking about.' She was like, 'Shut up. Just tell me.' I'm like, 'I honestly don't know'— I kept it going, even with her. And then she saw it. She was like, 'You're a jerk.'"

Between the two *Spider-Man* projects, Emma voiced a character in *The Croods* (2013) and reunited with Ryan Gosling in *Gangster Squad* (2013), her first action-thriller. It was based on the true story of LAPD officers who brought down a crime ring in 1949. Emma played Grace Faraday, a woman caught in a love triangle between gangster Mickey Cohen (Sean Penn) and police officer Sgt. Jerry Wooters (Ryan Gosling). In addition to bringing Stone and Gosling back together, the director, Ruben Fleischer, also directed *Zombieland*.

"Grace was a fictional character," Emma said in an interview posted on YouTube titled *Emma Stone on Grace*. "I'm lucky because I get to come up with a backstory instead of trying to play someone who actually existed."

Emma's character is motivated by the desire to be a star. While Emma had some of that motivation as a kid, getting into the character meant stretching her desire into obsession. She studied 1940s stars like Lauren Bacall and Vivien Leigh for inspiration.

In *Emma Stone on Grace*, Ruben Fleischer said, "I'm so lucky to get to work with Emma again. She's somebody you can't take your eyes off. And she's really developed as an actress ... she's an adult now, and I feel that really comes across in the film."

Then, Woody Allen came calling in 2014 and 2015.

Few would argue that Woody Allen is a problematic figure. Over his decades-long career, he has written, acted, and directed an astonishing number of award-winning films. He holds the title for the most nominations for the Academy Awards Best Original Screenplay and has won four Academy Awards, plus ten BAFTAs (British Academy Film and Television Awards), an Emmy, a Tony, and many other accolades. The films Woody Allen makes often achieve a legendary, even timeless, status, and he has launched many careers.

Emma plays Sophie in *Magic in the Moonlight* directed by Woody Allen in July 2014

THE TEEN COMEDY QUEEN EXPLORES NEW HORIZONS

When Emma Stone was interviewed by the *Guardian* after performing in her second film with Woody Allen, she was asked about the allegations stemming from his relationship with Soon-Yi Previn, the adopted daughter of his ex-wife Mia Farrow. Emma demurred, "There were two films in a row where the characters, for whatever reason, he wanted me to play them." She added that after filming they both moved on. "He's working with different people now."

The first of those two Woody Allen movies was *Magic in the Moonlight*, a 1920s period film. Emma portrays a medium who falls for a much older man, played by Colin Firth. The fact that Allen habitually pairs young women with older male romantic leads is deeply problematic because Allen married a woman thirty-five years his junior

Emma as Sophie Baker in *Magic in the Moonlight*, 2014

in the most public circumstances under the suspicion of abuse charges. In *Magic in the Moonlight*, Colin Firth's character was thirty years older than Emma's. For Emma's second Allen film, *Irrational Man*, Joaquin Phoenix's character is twenty years older than hers.

In that *Guardian* 2015 interview, Emma played off the age difference. Speaking of *Irrational Man*, she said that she relished the chance to act with Phoenix: "He's a truly brilliant actor." She went on to explain that the pairing fit the film. "Just to speak solely of *Irrational Man*, the relationship is genuinely a plot point," she said. "It's pretty openly discussed in the film that this is a student who is falling in love with her professor, and she wants to bring this intelligence and almost toxic energy into her life."

Magic in the Moonlight, 2014, starring Emma and Colin Firth

THE TEEN COMEDY QUEEN EXPLORES NEW HORIZONS

Before the *Guardian* interview ended, Emma added one last note about working with Woody Allen. "I'd also point out that in the next movie I did, with a completely different director, I was with somebody older than Joaquin, and that was never discussed."

That film was *Aloha* with Bradley Cooper, who is the same age as Joaquin Phoenix. "It's a Hollywood trope, that's what we need to discuss. It happens in many movies across the board, and that's definitely open for discussion," she said to the *Guardian*. "At least in *Irrational Man* it's brought attention to. I've been in other movies where attention is not brought to it at all."

Emma moved on from her two Woody Allen films, unaware that she would soon step, for the first time, into her own large-scale, public career controversy.

Irrational Man, 2015 directed by Woody Allen with Emma and Joaquin Phoenix

Emma (Jill Pollard) and Joaquin Phoenix (Abe Lucas) in *Irrational Man*, 2015

Emma starring in *Irrational Man*, 2015

THE TEEN COMEDY QUEEN EXPLORES NEW HORIZONS 73

ANOTHER HEROIC ROLE

In 2014, Emma stared in *Birdman* opposite Michael Keaton and Edward Norton. The film followed an actor, played by Michael Keaton, who had become famous for portraying a superhero (familiar territory for Michael, who had previously played Batman). Years later, he's trying to revive his career by starring in a Broadway play. Emma played the protagonist's estranged daughter, Sam.

Birdman won the Academy Awards for Best Picture and Best Original Screenplay and earned seven other nominations. Emma was nominated for Best Supporting Actress for her role as Sam.

In an interview with *Vulture* in 2014, Emma reflected on the experience and how her past movies provided the skills she needed for her *Birdman* role. "The only thing I felt that I had gained from *Spider-Man* was having no fear of heights," she related. "So, sitting on the roof

Emma playing Sam in *Birdman*, 2014

[of the St. James Theater], I was going over the edge, and Edward was terrified. He was like, 'Stop! Get back!' I was like, 'I am fine. It's four stories. It's nothing.' But they had a little harness clip on my shorts. They made me. I don't care! I like it."

In the 2015 awards season, Emma lost the Best Supporting Actress Academy Award to Julianne Moore for her role in *Still Alice*, but she was still in the spotlight at the awards show. Hosts Amy Poehler and Tina Fey used Emma as the punchline for one of their jokes.

Amy said, "Christoph Waltz and Amy Adams are here. They were so great in *Big Eyes*. In fact, one of those famous big-eye paintings is on display tonight." The camera then cut to Emma in the audience, and Tina exclaimed, "So lifelike! It's like it's cute, but it's creepy!"

Leaning into her improv skills, responding in the moment, Emma rolled her eyes, earning the laugh that she deserved.

Emma in *Birdman*, 2014, directed by Alejandro Gonzalez Iñárritu

THE TEEN COMEDY QUEEN EXPLORES NEW HORIZONS

Birdman cast and director: Andrea Riseborough, Alejandro Gonzalez Iñárritu, Emma, Naomi Watts, and Edward Norton backstage at the Oscars after winning Best Motion Picture of the Year, February 2015

Opposite: Emma at the *Birdman* premiere at the 71st Venice Film Festival, August 2014

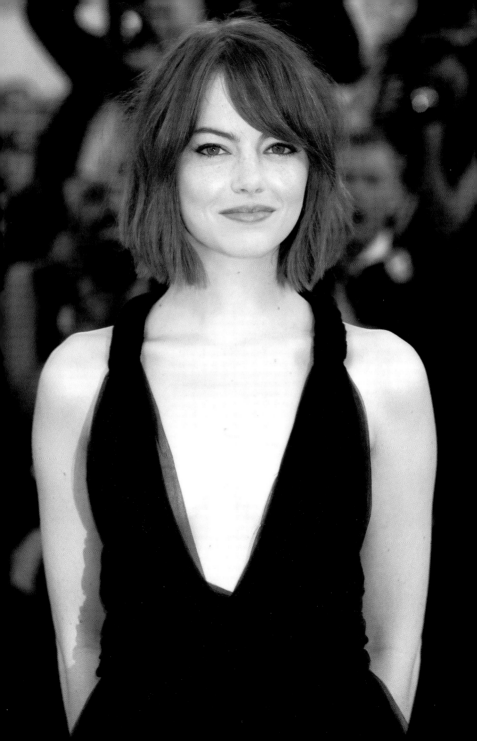

The SNL Society

For as long as she could recall, Emma Stone had dreamed of being on *Saturday Night Live*. Her wish first came true in 2010. In 2023, not only was she on the show again, but she was there to celebrate a milestone. It was her fifth appearance, bringing her into a club that included only five other women: Drew Barrymore, Melissa McCarthy, Scarlett Johansson, Candice Bergen, and Tina Fey. (The list of men is much longer, including performers like Will Ferrell, Ben Affleck, Steve Martin, and Tom Hanks.)

Emma's third hosting gig, in 2016, would become incredibly important in Emma's life. On the *SNL* set for that appearance, Emma met the man who would one day be her husband. Dave McCary wrote and directed Emma's sketch "Wells for Boys," and from that day forward, they worked to keep their relationship quiet for as long as they could.

As *InStyle* reported, "The two ended up hitting it off, but their relationship became one of Hollywood's best-kept secrets. It took nearly a year since they first met for everyone to realize they were dating and a whole year after that for them to make their couple debut."

Then in 2019, with musical guest BTS performing, the *SNL* cast gave Emma a four-timers jacket, which wasn't really a marker, since five was the magic number. The jacket was denim with the number four spray-painted on the back. The skit was a reminder of how close she was to the actual milestone.

When she finally received the correct jacket for her fifth hosting gig, musical guest Noah Kahan, Candice Bergen, and Tina Fey were on stage to present it. Emma feigned finding a joint in the pocket, and Tina and Candice declared it must've been Woody Harrelson's, but after they found a vaccine card in the jacket, they admitted they were wrong.

It's tradition that the guests return the five timer's jacket after the show. Only Emma didn't do that. She admitted to Jimmy Fallon that they did indeed ask for the jacket, but she ignored the ask. In 2024, *Entertainment Weekly* reported the exchange.

"They're like, 'You know you're not keeping the jacket. You're just wearing it for the monologue,'" she recalled. "I was like, 'No. I'll be taking it with me, I'll be wearing it to [the] after-party, and I'll be taking it home.'"

And she did just that. "I did take it home," Emma confessed through her laughter. "And now it's in my closet! That's right!"

With a final quip, she added, "They also know where to find me."

Not only does Emma live close to the NYC studio, but in 2020, she married David McCary, and so, finding her would be easy—her husband still worked at *SNL*.

chapter 4

Dramatic Depths

"I do remember saying to my mom, in the most dramatic sense possible . . . 'If I don't get to act, I will die.' Which is how I think you do know you're an actor: when it feels so dramatic, the idea that you wouldn't get to do it. It really solidifies the pain that you're in—[which,] as an actor, is worth it."

—Emma to *Backstage* in 2024

Cameron Crowe's 2015 film *Aloha* brought Emma into a movie-relationship with another older man. This time, her costar was Bradley Cooper. No one commented on the age gap between the two stars, but critics had a lot to say about the role Emma played.

In the film, Emma plays Allison Ng, a woman of Hawaiian and Asian heritage. Emma is neither, so the choice to cast her in the role (and for her to accept it) seemed odd to many, regardless of how well Emma may have played the character. Crowe responded to the

Emma attending the 61st BFI London Film Festival in London, England, October 2017 controversy in a blog post, saying, "Thank you so much for all the impassioned comments regarding the casting of the wonderful Emma Stone in the part of Allison Ng. I have heard your words and your disappointment, and I offer you a heartfelt apology to all who felt this was an odd or misguided casting choice."

Crowe went on to praise Emma for her character choices and the incredible amount of research she did before taking on the role.

In the same posting, he added, "I am grateful for the dialogue. And from the many voices, loud and small, I have learned something very inspiring. So many of us are hungry for stories with more racial diversity, more truth in representation, and I am anxious to help tell those stories in the future."

Sony, the film's studio, also felt the need to reply. As reported in the *Guardian*, the studio defended the choice: "While some have been

Emma and Bradley Cooper starring in *Aloha* in 2015

quick to judge a movie they haven't seen and a script they haven't read, the film *Aloha* respectfully showcases the spirit and culture of the Hawaiian people."

Emma herself responded, as well, when interviewed by an Australian news site. "I've become the butt of many jokes," she said, referring to her role in *Aloha*. "I've learned on a macro level about the insane history of whitewashing in Hollywood and how prevalent the problem truly is. It's ignited a conversation that's very important."

At the 2019 Golden Globes, the controversy lingered. Host Sandra Oh joked about it in her opening monologue, saying, "[*Crazy Rich Asians*] is the first studio film with an Asian American lead since *Ghost in the Shell* and *Aloha*." (The 2017 film *Ghost in the Shell* starred Scarlett Johansson as a Japanese character in a manga remake.)

In response to Sandra Oh, Emma shouted, "Oh, I'm sorry!" Her voice echoed through the crowd.

Emma playing Allison Ng in the movie *Aloha*, 2015

DRAMATIC DEPTHS

After a quick cameo in 2016's *Popstar: Never Stop Stopping*, Emma's next film brought her wide acclaim, and the chance to return to her roots in musical theater.

In 2016's *La La Land*, Emma sang and danced alongside costar Ryan Gosling. When she was interviewed about the movie by *E!* that year, Emma was asked about how the film made her feel. "The movie takes you to people struggling in LA, trying to make it as an actor. Did it take you back to your time when you first came to town?"

Emma replied, "Yeah, absolutely. That was a very cathartic and, you know, interesting part, playing Mia, and Ryan and I told Damien some of our audition stories, so he was nice enough to utilize some of those."

When speaking to *Vanity Fair* that same year, Emma dove deeper: "You sort of have this set kind of family and environment for a couple months at a time and then you move on to either nothing or an entirely different family and location and place in the world. So, it's this sort of endless, I mean, especially early on when you're auditioning, there's

Emma looking regal in cobalt in *La La Land*, 2016.

Following: Emma and Ryan Gosling in *La La Land*, 2016

EMMA

all these different characters that you're trying to play. If you're lucky, five or six different characters per week, if you're getting that many auditions. And you're putting yourself in all these different headspaces and worlds. And then to actually make these things, it still is an ever-changing thing that falls away time and time again. But I think that's what's exciting about it for me is that you're not stuck in one place for a long period of time. You're always kind of exploring and growing and changing. And that's sort of what I love about it, even though that is also the hardest part."

Ryan Gosling also remarked on the Hollywood audition process, "Obviously we set ourselves up, as actors, for a lot of rejection, but I don't think that's something specific to us. I mean, it feels like everybody is facing—no one knows really what tomorrow's going to bring."

When *La La Land* opened at the Venice Film Festival in 2016, the audience began applauding after the first ten minutes of the film. That shot of support set the stage for the movie's global reception. Emma won both the Academy Award and the BAFTA for Best Actress in a Leading Role. Overall, the movie was nominated for fourteen Academy Awards and took home six. In a historic moment, Faye Dunaway looked at the card announcing the Best Picture that year and noticed Emma Stone's name. She thought that meant that *La La Land* had won Best Picture and announced it. The cast and crew flooded on stage, celebrating with their speeches. It took a full two minutes before the mistake was identified: Warren Beatty had given Faye Dunaway the wrong card. *La La Land* was not the big winner that year; the top film prize went to *Moonlight*.

PricewaterhouseCoopers, the accounting house responsible for the announcements, said in a statement, "We sincerely apologize to *Moonlight*, *La La Land*, Warren Beatty, Faye Dunaway, and Oscar viewers for the error that was made during the award announcement for best picture. We appreciate the grace with which the nominees, the academy, ABC, and [host] Jimmy Kimmel handled the situation."

"You're always kind of **exploring** and **growing** and **changing**. And that's sort of what I love about [making movies], even though that is also the **hardest part.**"

For his part, Jimmy Kimmel quipped, "I blame Steve Harvey," the comedian who fumbled announcing the correct winner at the 2015 Miss Universe pageant.

Backstage at the Oscars, Emma was asked about the mix-up by a reporter from *Variety Magazine*.

"Is that the craziest Oscar moment of all time?" Emma replied. When the reporters all agreed, yes it was, she went on, "Cool! I guess we made history tonight. I don't even know what to say. I was still on such a buzzy train backstage that I was on another planet already. This felt like another planet. I think it's an incredible outcome but a very strange happening for Oscar history."

With *La La Land*'s acting Oscar win on the shelf, Emma continued to find rich roles to play.

Emma at the 89th Annual Academy Awards in Hollywood, California, February 2017

HISTORIC ROLES

The *LAist* interviewed Emma in 2017 about the challenge she faced playing tennis icon Billie Jean King in *Battle of the Sexes*.

"I wanted to know as much as possible about her story, definitely," she explained. "It was helpful for me to really try and key into her in that exact time period, rather than the kind of circumspection that she has now, where she has forty-ish years distance from that time period and her life. So, it was amazing to watch interviews or read articles of her back then, the way she was presenting herself, the sound of her voice back then, which is different than it is now . . . I could feel a lot of changes within her from then to now."

Emma also learned about acting from Billie Jean King. "One of the greatest things she did as a good coach—which she is—is right when I met her, she said, 'What do you like to do the most?'" Emma said of the icon. "I said, 'I like to act, I like to read, I like to dance.' She said, 'Well, this is dancing. That's all this is. This is my stage, the court is my stage, I am a performer, and that's what I'm feeling the entire time.' So we relate completely on that."

The film brought Emma and her costar Steve Carell (also in *Crazy, Stupid, Love*) Golden Globe nominations, but for Emma, the lasting impact was greater than any award. In that same *LAist* interview, she said, "These are the shoulders on which we stand. Someone like Billie Jean is such a huge part of our country's history and LGBTQ history, and there's just so much that she's done. It's just an honor to tell that story and to introduce it to a generation like mine. My generation was not around for this match and has heard of Billie Jean, but maybe doesn't understand the extent of this fight. And I think it's really important to know who has come before us to get us to where we are today and hopefully galvanize within us now."

Emma and Steve Carell starring in *Battle of the Sexes*, 2017

"These are the shoulders on which we stand. Someone like Billie Jean [King] is such a huge part of our country's history and LGBTQ history, and there's just so much that she's done. It's just an honor to tell that story and to introduce it to a generation like mine."

Emma (as Billie Jean King) and Andrea Riseborough (as Marilyn Barnett) on the set of *Battle of the Sexes*, 2017

Following: Emma and Billie Jean King at the premiere of *Battle of the Sexes* during the 61st BFI London Film Festival, October 2017

But it wasn't just history that impacted Emma in this film. The role made her introspective as well. She told *Forbes*, "Sometimes I worry about all the mistakes I have made. I think about the choices, the things I could do different, and I beat myself up about it. But then, with this movie, I realized that there could be so much going on with you every day, and you can be afraid and be flawed and be imperfect, but you can also have the courage and have a voice to speak out for what is right and keep growing and changing. I feel like I am on my way to being braver and more courageous, and I thank Billie Jean for that."

DRAMATIC DEPTHS 91

"I feel like I am on my way to being braver and more courageous, and I thank Billie Jean for that."

Behind the scenes of *The Favourite*, directed by Yorgos Lanthimos and starring Emma in 2018

Next on the docket was *The Favourite*, a 2018 film by Yorgos Lanthimos. Emma had wanted to work with the director since seeing his films *The Lobster* and *The Killing of a Sacred Deer*. The *Independent* summed up their relationship by saying, "They've rapidly formed one of the movies' strongest director-actor partnerships, a collaboration based on a shared sense of absurdity and a willingness to go, full-tilt, to some very strange places."

When *The Favourite* came along, Emma was at a career level where she got work without auditions, and yet, she was willing to audition to play Abigail to show Yorgos what she could do. Emma told *Collider* that when she read the script, she immediately knew she wanted that role. The interviewer asked when Emma had last auditioned for a role, and she had to think about it. After a pause, Emma replied, "It's different than the auditions that I was doing when I first moved to LA. It's kind of like, okay, we've seen you do stuff before, but we need to hear you sing or we need to hear your accent, or you know it's that kind of thing."

While she told *Backstage Experience* that the role of Abigail was physically demanding, she also declared that it was worth it. "Yeah,

Emma playing Abigail in *The Favourite*, 2018

you know, falling down, smacking, tackling, all of that constantly being whipped, you know, it was just every day was a different pain."

There was an additional pain the actor had to endure for the role: her corset caused her "organs to shift." As Emma explained to the *Hollywood Reporter* in 2018, "After about a month, my organs shifted because they have to. It was only temporary, but it was gross. The bottom half of my stomach, whatever, I'm not a doctor, whatever is in there, went down that way, and I guess just my ribs stayed up."

After *The Favourite* wrapped (and Emma's organs returned to normal), she was eager to work for Yorgos again. The respect for the Greek art-house filmmaker took her from this role to two other features with him, plus one short film in 2022. In an interview with the *Independent UK*, she considered why she was drawn to Yorgos's filmmaking, saying, "The common denominator of the things I've been a part of are that they're things I want to watch. That's the only gauge that I have. If it's not something that I would be like, 'I gotta go see this the day it comes out,' then it's probably not a good fit for me."

DRAMATIC DEPTHS 95

Speaking to *Indiewire* in 2024, Emma went on to explain her great respect for Yorgos and his art. "I think the elements of control are in everything he's ever done. That's, I think, an obsession of his and something very interesting to him—human nature and the kinds of agreements we make about socialization and what we're supposed to be," she said. "Who's in charge? Do we want to be in charge of ourselves or do we want someone else to be? What does it mean to be loved? These are all these abstract, strange, surrealistic depictions, these things that are very human and affect us all."

In return, Yorgos told *W* in 2023, "There is absolutely nothing that Emma cannot do. She is fearless."

Before Emma returned to work with Yorgos again in 2022 and 2023, she revisited her past and filmed the sequel to *Zombieland*. *Zombieland: Double Tap* brought Emma back onto set with Woody Harrelson, who Emma told *Fandango* would be the best zombie warrior. But for Emma, the film was more about relationships than zombies.

In an interview posted on the FilmIsNow Movie Bloopers & Extras YouTube channel, she explained, "I think it's really a story about making your own family. . . . I think the deeper message, even in something like *Zombieland*, is that, you know, horrible things have happened, or feels like the world is falling apart, you do kind of create your family and you do choose people that you love and you want to stick with and that's what these four people have done."

The one thing that Emma avoided on the sequel set was the pulled muscle she experienced the first time around. As she explained to *Collider* in 2009, "I'm shockingly terrible at action movies. I tore my muscle three days in [on the first *Zombieland*], just running, and then I was limping around everywhere. [Rhett] Reese [one of the creators and cowriters] had to push through it because I was limping like a zombie. [Laughter] I'm dead serious. We're running from zombies, and I'm limping in the same fashion that they limp. It was just awful. I just had to try and rally, and I don't know that I did it that well. It's been really fun and really different to learn to shoot guns and to try and look tough."

Zombieland: Double Tap with Jesse Eisenberg, Woody Harrelson, Abigail Breslin, and Emma, 2019

Emma showing force in *Zombieland: Double Tap*, 2019

Following: A scene from *The Favourite* staring Emma, 2018

DRAMATIC DEPTHS 97

"The common denominator of the things I've been a part of are that they're things I want to watch. That's the only gauge that I have."

The cast of *Zombieland* at the Chinese Theater premiere in Los Angeles, California, September 2009

"I think it's really a story about making your own family.... I think the deeper message, even in something like *Zombieland*, is that, you know, horrible things have happened, or feels like the world is falling apart, you do kind of create your family and you do choose people that you love and you want to stick with and that's what these four people have done."

Emma as Cruella de Vil in Disney's *Cruella*, 2021

THE FRUIT TREE

In the spring of 2020, Emma and husband Dave McCary founded their own production company, Fruit Tree. They took on a project with Jesse Eisenberg, her friend from *Zombieland*. Eisenberg told *IndieWire*, "Producing is overwhelming work, and they were starting to do it during a pandemic. I was impressed that these two brilliant people wanted to talk logistics and budgets and stuff."

In 2021, Emma starred in *Cruella* as the titular Disney villain and also served as executive producer on the film. *Glamour* asked her how it felt to play a "baddie." Emma replied, "When you think no one has to like me, in fact I'd prefer if they didn't—I just want what I want, I am single-minded—it is an incredible feeling. Not something that you can really live in in real life for very long at all, hopefully."

DRAMATIC DEPTHS

Emma crashing the party and, as always, doing it in style in *Cruella*, 2021

Opposite: Emma (Cruella de Vil) performing a scene in Disney's *Cruella*, 2021

Cruella wasn't Emma's first taste of work behind the camera. Her first producer credit was on Cary Fukunaga's Netflix miniseries *Maniac* in 2018. She both portrayed the character of Annie Landsberg, a woman struggling with addiction, and worked behind the scenes, adding her voice to the tone and vision of the series. As an actor, she was able to show the character's trauma in this dark portrayal. As a producer, she was key in major decisions including the casting of Jonah Hill, who she'd worked with in *Superbad*.

Emma told *IndieWire* in 2022 that she truly appreciated balancing both roles. "As an actor, you usually just go with what comes to you and you're at the mercy of the process. We don't want to say we just want to make things—that sounds trite. Because we have these long-standing relationships, we thought it would be amazing to support these people in a more meaningful way than just being a cog."

Emma now moves fluidly from in front of a camera to behind the scenes. When she returned to working with Yorgos Lanthimos in 2023, on the film *Poor Things*, she both took on the role of Bella Baxter and came onboard as a producer. The decision would turn out to be one of the best she'd ever made.

Danny Burstein, Emma, and Alan Cumming onstage during Emma's debut performance in Broadway's *Cabaret* in New York City, New York, November 2014

Roundabout Theatre Marquee for Emma's debut performance in *Cabaret*, November 2014

Come to the Cabaret

In 2014, Emma Stone starred in the revival of *Cabaret* at the Roundabout Theater in New York City. This version of the Kander and Ebb musical revisited Sam Mendes's 1993 production. Michelle Williams opened the show in the role of Sally Bowles, but in February 2014, Emma took on the challenging role. The show follows Sally, an English singer at the Kit-Kat Club, navigating the rise of the Third Reich in Berlin in 1929. The singing and dancing are intentionally risqué, and the musical uses the bawdy entertainment of the time to highlight the prejudice and authoritarianism running rampant with the rise of Nazism.

The musical originated on Broadway in 1966 and won the 1967 Tony Awards for Best Musical and Best Original Score. The 1972 movie, based on the stage show, propelled Liza Minelli into the spotlight with an Oscar win for Best Actress. The film also earned an additional eight Oscars.

When Emma joined the cast in 2014, she knew she was stepping into a famous show and dancing in the footsteps of illustrious stars. In 2024, *Broadway World* asked her about the experience, and Emma admitted that she wasn't sure she'd do another show.

DRAMATIC DEPTHS

"I never thought it was going to be easy," she explained. "But I was like, 'It's three hours a day, you're just doing it at night. You're gonna hang out all day, you go, you do the show, you go home.' You literally have to live like a monk. Your voice is always gone, or at least mine because of my voice, it's broken." But, the actor added, "I will tell you; it did make me fall in love with acting in a whole new way."

Variety reviewed Emma's performance in December 2014. "While Stone is even less of a singer than Williams, she acts her way out of every tight spot. When Sally dares to hope that there's a future for her and Cliff, Stone makes 'Maybe This Time' a cry that comes right from the heart. And when those hopes turn to ashes, Stone pours all that pain and rage and despair into her electrifying delivery of 'Cabaret.' Not too shabby for a non-singer, and exactly what you'd expect from a real actor."

It wouldn't be long before Emma took what she'd learned from *Cabaret* into her 2016 role in *La La Land*, winning herself, and the film, international praise.

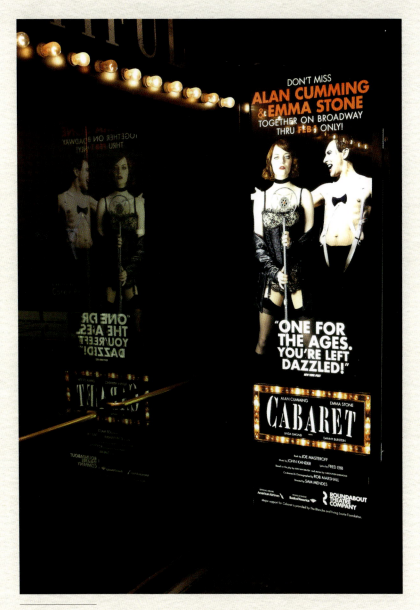

Emma and Alan Cumming in *Cabaret* on Broadway, New York City, New York, November 2014

chapter 5

Balancing Career, Family, and Friendships

"I do find that I'm drawn to people in my life, romantically or not, that have something to teach me. I'm drawn to people who I feel like I can learn from. I'm not really drawn to toxic people—I don't find myself discovering that someone in my life is toxic very often. But there is some sense of being changed by each person that I think I'm drawn to."

—Emma talking to Cameron Crowe for *Interview Magazine* in 2012

Emma Stone met Dave McCary on the set of *Saturday Night Live* when she was hosting in 2016. For a long time, they kept their relationship quiet, until a fan caught the two of them at a premiere for *Brigsby Bear*—a film Dave directed—and posted a video. Neither Emma nor Dave officially responded to the video or the post.

Emma with Dave McCary at the Vanity Fair Oscar Party in Beverly Hills, California, March 2024

Emma and Dave at the LA Clippers basketball game in Los Angeles, California, January 2019

Later in 2017, a "source" close to both revealed that they had indeed been dating for about three months. That news was confirmed in *People* but didn't go much further in the gossip mill.

When Emma went to the Golden Globes alone in 2019, there was speculation that the relationship had ended, but a few weeks later, she and Dave appeared at a Los Angeles Clippers game together. From there, sightings of the couple increased, and fans were interested in where the relationship was headed.

In the spring of 2019, a photo appeared of Emma wearing a pearl and diamond ring. But it wasn't until many months later that McCary himself posted a photo about their engagement, showing off her pearl ring. Soon after, they bought a house in Malibu together.

COVID brought new challenges, and the couple postponed their wedding plans publicly. But three months later, Emma was seen wearing a gold band. Their wedding, like their relationship, had been a private affair. It wasn't until September 2020 that *People* was able to quote a source saying the two were indeed married.

Through it all, Emma was working, winning awards, and growing her career. Having finished *The Favourite* with Yorgos Lanthimos in 2018, the opportunity to work with him again came in 2022. *Bleat* was a silent film shot in Greece. In a video shoot for the New York Film Festival, Emma said, "It was so beautiful . . . We shot this in February of 2020 right before the pandemic . . . and knowing that there wasn't any dialogue, you just got to sort of, you know, live in the landscape of this incredible place. It was magical. I would like to make more short films that are silent."

Emma hasn't done another silent film yet, but her friendship with Yorgos Lanthimos would bring them back together for *Poor Things* in 2023. But first, her future plans would undergo a major change.

In an interview with Jennifer Lawrence for *Elle* in 2018, Emma revealed that her thoughts about having children had changed. "As a teenager, I was like, I'm never getting married, I'm never having kids," she said. "And then I got older, and I was like, I really want to get married, I really want to have kids."

It took four years to develop *Poor Things* and, in that time, Emma and Dave had a baby. Louise Jean was born in March 2021. The baby's name is a tribute to Jean Louise, Emma's grandmother.

When Emma returned to work, *Poor Things* was consuming, but her baby and her family were always on her mind. A source told *Us Weekly* in 2023, "She's able to bring Louise to the set with her and that makes a huge difference." Additionally, "There is no shortage of people in her circle willing to help with Louise—and Emma is grateful to them." The anonymous source also mentioned that husband Dave was "hands-on."

Speaking to *Good Morning America* in 2024, Emma recounted, "I started talking to Yorgos about this movie in 2017 and I had her [Louise Jean] in 2021 when we were about to make the movie. So, it was kind of a crazy confluence of events. But she was only five months old when we went to start shooting it, so it was incredible to get to be there with her."

Following: Emma playing the role of Bella Baxter in *Poor Things,* directed by Yorgos Lanthimos, September 2023

"We had **talked** about the **film** and the way it would be done for so long, and I believed **so deeply** in **Bella** not having this **shame**. The camera didn't need to have that **shame either**."

With her child well cared for, Emma was free to dive deep into her *Poor Things* character. A reporter unpacked the experience of filming the new project with *CBS Sunday Morning*, explaining, "Lanthimos breaks down inhibitions by having cast members play theater games and rehearsals, rather than just read through the script. And he likes to keep his set quiet." The reporter pressed him by asking, "You don't yell action?" In his quiet manner, he replied, "In general we try to create this atmosphere which doesn't create tension."

Emma appreciated this calm, especially as *Poor Things* required Emma to be naked, as her character, Bella, is experiencing life for the first time. Those new experiences often include sex, which Bella calls "furious jumping." In 2024, Emma told *Screen Daily*, "We had talked about the film and the way it would be done for so long, and I believed so deeply in Bella not having this shame. The camera didn't need to have that shame either. She's a very free being who doesn't understand she's supposed to feel the need to cover up. And it was a closed set, and

A scene from *Poor Things*, starring Emma (Bella Baxter), September 2023

we had this amazing intimacy coordinator who made it feel very safe."

When *Poor Things* won the Golden Lion, the highest prize at the Venice Film Festival, Emma couldn't attend because of the SAG strike that summer. She told *Screen Daily*, "I was devastated. The strike was incredibly necessary, and I'm so glad we fought for what we needed, but the idea of this film coming out when it was going to originally was killing me." After a personal campaign, the film's release date was changed until the strike ended. In the same interview, she said, "I'm so grateful I've gotten to be out here in support of it. I don't know if it's helpful. Selfishly, I just want to be around for everything." By changing the release date, Emma was able to go out on interviews and celebrate the success of the movie.

The film was nominated for and won many awards, with Emma herself taking home the 2024 Golden Globe and Academy Award for Best Actress. Because Emma was nominated as an actor at the Academy Awards and the film was also nominated for Best Picture, with

Emma as newborn yet fashionable Bella Baxter, pondering life in 2023's *Poor Things*

BALANCING CAREER, FAMILY, AND FRIENDSHIPS

Emma as one of the producers, Emma made history as only the second woman to be nominated for both roles on the same film.

In her Best Actress Academy Award speech, Emma gave a rare, intimate tribute to her family. "I really just want to thank my family—my mom; my brother, Spencer; my dad; my husband, Dave. I love you so much. And most importantly, my daughter, who's going to be three in three days, who has turned our lives technicolor." Her speech was punctuated with tears. "I love you bigger than the whole sky, my girl, so thank you so much."

As of November 2024, her career shows no signs of slowing down, with filming already complete on Yorgos Lanthimos's next film, *Kinds of Kindness*, and her series, *The Curse*, having premiered on Showtime. She's also busy with the production company she and her husband own.

As an anonymous source told *Us Weekly*, "For Emma, quitting acting and being a stay-at-home mom would be like cutting off one of her limbs. That's just not her. Acting is as vital to her as breathing, it's a part of who she is—and Dave's 100 percent behind her."

Emma and Joe Alwyn in *Kinds of Kindness*, directed by Yorgos Lanthimos, June 2024

Opposite: Emma at the Cannes Film Festival in Cannes, France, May 2015

KEEPING FRIENDS CLOSE

Emma Stone's friends aren't surprised by her success. In addition to Andrew Garfield, who calls himself her "biggest fan," Emma's list of close confidants includes Ryan Gosling, Jennifer Lawrence, and Taylor Swift.

After having performed in three movies with Ryan, Emma called him a friend. At the Telluride Film Festival Q and A in Colorado, Emma said, "I can't even imagine what my life would be without Ryan. He's so special. It makes me emotional. He's so talented but he's such a great person to work with because he's so collaborative and excited about the process. He's taught me a lot about being really generous."

When Ryan performed at the 2024 Academy Awards—during which Emma would win Best Actress for *Poor Things*—Emma danced so wildly to her friend's performance of "I'm Just Ken" from *Barbie* that she broke the zipper in her dress.

After hearing her name called for the award, she walked onto the stage, revealing to the presenters and the audience, "My dress is broken." She later explained, "I was really excited for Ryan. He just absolutely crushed it, and it was a blast. So, it was worth the dress rip."

Emma has that kind of mutual enthusiasm for all her friends. In 2024, *Elle* posted an article called, "How Emma Stone and Jennifer Lawrence went from Rivals to Best Friends." The article detailed how Jennifer Lawrence had also auditioned for *Easy A*, which Jennifer told *The Hollywood Reporter*, "I wanted it so bad." Lawrence didn't list other films, but had previously mentioned that they often auditioned for the same roles. Looking back on those days, she joked to *Vanity Fair*, "If I weren't her biggest fan, I would've Tonya Harding'd her in the kneecaps."

Meanwhile, Emma saw Jennifer racking up early film successes in *Winter's Bone* and *The Hunger Games*. Emma recalled how that felt to *Vanity Fair* as well: "Oh, hey, my ego is going nuts, she's so great and vibrant and talented, I'm screwed, I'll never work again."

Emma and Taylor Swift at the Teen Choice Awards in Universal City, California, August 2011

Following: Emma and Ryan Gosling at the 74th Annual Golden Globes in Beverly Hills, California, January 2017

"I can't even imagine what my life would be without Ryan. He's so special. It makes me emotional."

In 2013, the two finally met—though not as colleagues on a film set, but because they shared an admirer—of sorts. They reached out to one another with stories about "John the Orchestra Guy," who, as Emma explained in *W*'s "Best Performances" feature, "He wasn't really a stalker. He's just this guy who has a lot of people's phone numbers. He must have worked at a studio or something." John would accidentally text both of them, telling them he was late to work, or to "warm up the

Emma with Jennifer Lawrence at the Academy of Motion Pictures Arts and Sciences 9th Annual Governors Awards in Hollywood, California, November 2017

orchestra." When Emma and Jennifer finally met, they realized what had happened, and their fears dissipated. Friendship blossomed.

In 2018, Emma invited Jennifer to be her date for the Golden Globes after-party. But then, just before the car came for Jennifer, Emma backed out. In a video posted to Facebook, Jennifer recalled, "You had told me that you wanted me to be your date to the after-parties, so I got us tickets to some after-parties, I booked a car, and I was halfway through glam when you told me that you didn't want to go. You just wanted to come over to my house. So, I sent my hair and makeup team home."

Jennifer turned her face to show only one side made up. She laughed. "And now this is what I look like."

To which Emma replied, "You're the best."

Emma and Jennifer seek out time to be together during their demanding work schedules. In a fun twist of fate, the two also both gave birth in the same year. Their relationship is so special that it was an amazing moment when Jennifer was on stage as Emma's name was called for the 2024 *Poor Things* Oscar. It was incredible . . . and confusing.

Four women, all of whom had won the Best Actress Award in the past, stood on stage at that moment: Michelle Yeoh, Charlize Theron, Sally Field, and Jennifer Lawrence. Michelle Yeoh was holding the trophy. In an awkward exchange, Michelle looked like she was going to hand Jennifer the trophy instead of Emma, having seemingly confused the two actors. In truth, Michelle was eager for Jennifer to join her so that they could deliver the award together.

The next day, the confusion was cleared up. Michelle posted on Instagram: "Congratulations Emma!! I confused you, but I wanted to share that glorious moment of handing over Oscar to you together with your best friend Jennifer!! She reminded me of my Bae Jamie Lee Curtis 💙✨ always there for each other!! 😘😘"

During a conversation with Jimmy Fallon in 2024, another of Emma's special friendships came to light. Jimmy mentioned the gifts that she made for her friends during COVID, and how he'd been fortunate to receive one. He showed Emma and the audience the present, which he keeps in a ziplock bag.

"You made me a bracelet once. Did you remember making me this?" he asked. "Was this during the pandemic? It says, 'Bracelet for Jimmy.'"

Emma laughed and turned to the audience. "Well, yeah, you guys probably all, you know, like, remember COVID where everybody got a hobby? Where it was like, 'I'll make sourdough.'"

Jimmy replied, "This was your jam?"

Emma smiled. "I was making bracelets and so, yeah."

Despite their prevalence on the Eras Tour, it's unclear if Taylor Swift received an Emma-made friendship bracelet, but the two have been close friends since 2008. Emma explained to *MTV News* that they first met in 2008 at *Hollywood Life Magazine's* Young Hollywood Awards. Emma claims that after that meeting, she pursued the friendship. "We met there three years ago, and then I listened to some of her music, and I wrote her an e-mail saying I liked her music, I swear. And then we started talking and hanging out."

All through 2009, Taylor @taylorswift13 was seen publicly tweeting to Emma at @ijustmight.

March 29, 2009
@ijustmight I saw a vintage sweater with a cat on it today and thought of you. Very few other people could pull off such hipness.

May 18, 2009
@ijustmight I'm using every form of communication to reach you. Call me dude. I knitted you a crochet hat.

In December 2009, *Just Jared* posted a photo of the two stars getting ice cream. Taylor later tweeted about the night: "Photo shoot all day, followed by dinner with Emma Stone. Then we wandered around a candy store like wide-eyed little kids."

Taylor attended the premiere of *Easy A*. The next year, she and Emma were seen together at the 2011 Met Gala. That same year, Emma got a sneak peek at Taylor's third album, *Speak Now*. Emma told *MTV News*, "I was lucky enough to hear it pretty early on, so it's so exciting for it to be out and own the songs instead of just be singing them [in my head]. Taylor's a pretty normal girl. She's not [like], 'I am one of the world's most popular singers.'"

In 2011, Emma presented Taylor with a surfboard at the Teen Choice Awards for Choice Female Artist. The following year, Taylor told *Access Hollywood* about her friendships with both Emma and Selena Gomez: "It's just so important to have people that you trust, and Emma and Selena and I, we've had so many things in our lives that have changed over the last couple years, but our friendship has stayed the same. So that's really good."

Emma with Taylor Swift at the Chinese Theatre for the *Easy A* premiere in Hollywood, California, September 2010

BALANCING CAREER, FAMILY, AND FRIENDSHIPS

Taylor caught her friend in the Broadway production of *Cabaret* in 2014, and when Taylor was dating Joe Alwyn, he starred in *The Favourite* with Emma. More recently, Emma went to the Eras Tour in Glendale, California, and caught it again in Las Vegas a few months later. Emma told *Vanity Fair*, "The concert was pretty amazing. I was lucky 'cause we've been friends for a really long time. I've known her since we were seventeen and eighteen, so she hooked me up, which was very nice 'cause I know those tickets are impossible to get. She's a wonderful friend."

The interviewer asked if a duet was in the friends' futures, to which Emma replied, "Oh, God, hell no! I can't sing, like, for a massive stadium. Let's not even go down that road. She has insane talent—I could never do what she does."

In an offbeat and misunderstood 2024 interview, after Emma won her Golden Globe for *Poor Things*, Emma was asked about her friendship with Taylor. Audiences and fans had noticed Taylor clapping wildly for Emma. Taylor had also been nominated for her own massive box office hit, *Taylor Swift: The Eras Tour Concert Film*.

Emma is often silly and impulsive around her friends. She leaned into this humor, without thinking about how it would be received publicly, when she joked with reporters, "What an asshole. I've known her for almost twenty years. I was very happy she was there, and she was also nominated tonight, which was wonderful. And yes, what an asshole."

The backlash was immediate and fierce. When the dust settled, Emma told *Variety*, "I definitely won't make a joke like that again . . . because I saw headlines that really pulled it out of context." She shook her head at her own mistake, and pointed to herself, saying, "What a dope."

Emma and TayTay Tell All

Taylor Swift's 2024 album *The Tortured Poets Society* contains several hints to her friendship with Emma Stone. Or does it?

A deep dive into the liner notes for a track entitled "Florida!!!," which features Florence and the Machine, also includes the name Emily Jean Stone, the birth name of the artist now known as Emma Stone. The mysterious Emily Jean is credited with "oddities." No other song has a similar listing.

Upon release, rumors swirled regarding the notation. It's possible that Emma attended the recording of the song and contributed "odd" sounds. Perhaps she cheered? Or talked? Or even coughed? However, as *Entertainment Weekly* noted, when guests add those kinds of sounds, they are often credited. For example, on Taylor's track "I Can Do It With a Broken Heart," the credits read "Talking by Oli Jacobs." If Emma provided similar sounds, wouldn't she be credited in the same fashion? The reason behind Emma's credit on "Florida!!!" remains unclear, but this is not Emma's only connection to Taylor's music.

Taylor is known for her open heart and public life. She writes songs about past loves, current loves, friends, and enemies. In 2023, she revealed a track list for *Speak Now*. On the list were six unreleased tracks, "from the vault." One of those was "When Emma Falls in Love."

The internet got to work. Who was "Emma"? Possibilities included Emma Watson from the *Harry Potter* movies or Jane Austen's novel *Emma* (or its titular character). Some suspected it could be a random "Emma" that Taylor met along the way. Or could this "Emma" be Taylor's good friend Emma Stone?

When Taylor Swift performed in Kansas City, she introduced the song by saying, "I wrote about one of my best friends." There was nothing more said. This brief statement seemed like confirmation that the track was indeed about Emma Stone.

There are a number of clues, which *Entertainment Weekly* outlined in 2023. For example, at the song's start, Taylor sings that when Emma falls in love, the first person she calls is her mom. It's well-known that Emma Stone has a close relationship with her mom, even taking her to awards shows as her plus-one. Additionally, Emma is committed to breast cancer charities, especially since her mother's diagnosis and remission. The lyrics also refer to the song's Emma as "Little Miss Sunshine," which fans quickly connected to Emma Stone's performance of "Pocketful of Sunshine" in *Easy A*. Taylor attended the premiere of that film with Emma.

The *Entertainment Weekly* article was published the day before Taylor's introduction of the song in Kansas City. The magazine quickly added an editor's note to the article: "The day after this story was published, Swift performed the song during the acoustic set of her Eras Tour stop in Kansas City where she told the audience the song was written about one of her best friends. We rest our case."

Good friends, Emma and Taylor Swift, posing for a photo in West Hollywood, California, February 2011

BALANCING CAREER, FAMILY, AND FRIENDSHIPS 129

chapter 6

Cementing Critical Acclaim

"Success is such a fleeting thing. I've seen how the careers of people I look up to ebb and flow, so I don't get carried away by it."

—Emma quoted in the *Daily Express* in 2012

Emma Stone is quite the decorated performer. Not only has she won two Academy Awards, but she also marked Academy Award history as one of only two actresses to be nominated for Best Actress and Best Picture in the same year. (The other was Frances McDormand for *Nomadland*.)

Early in her career, Emma earned the Young Hollywood Award for Exciting New Face. This award, for 2007's *Superbad*, set the ball rolling. For *Zombieland*, she was nominated for the Teen Choice Award for Choice Movie Actress: Comedy. The film also earned her a Best

---

Emma wins Best Actress in a Leading Role award for *Poor Things*, Hollywood, California, March 2024

Emma giving an acceptance speech at the Life Magazine's 10th Annual Young Hollywood Awards, April 2008

Ensemble Award at the 2010 Scream Awards, as well as a nomination for Best Horror Actress at the same awards show.

Easy A propelled her to more trophies and nominations. She was nominated for both the BAFTA Rising Star and the Golden Globe Award for Best Actress in a Musical or Comedy. Her role won her the MTV Movie Award for Best Comedic Performance.

That same year, Emma was selected to be in *TIME*'s list of "Top 10 of Everything of 2010." Journalist Richard Corliss noted that while *Easy A* was "OK," Emma's performance was "winning." He wrote, "This twenty-two-year-old is an actress-personality—a star—around whom Hollywood could build some pretty good movies. Katherine Heigl, watch your back."

Emma winning the Best Comedic Performance award at the MTV Movie Awards, June 2011

CEMENTING CRITICAL ACCLAIM 133

From *Easy A* forward, Emma continued to collect accolades. Teen Choice Award nominations came her way after *Crazy, Stupid, Love*; *The Help*; and *The Amazing Spider-Man*. For *Spider-Man*, her portrayal of Gwen Stacy also nabbed her a nomination for Choice Summer Movie Star: Female.

In 2017, *Birdman* earned Emma her first Academy Award nomination, as well as recognition by the BAFTAs, the Golden Globes, the Screen Actors Guild Awards, and the MTV Awards. But it was her role in *La La Land* that brought the star her first Academy Award win. At the ceremony, Emma was overwhelmed by her Best Actress prize and showed great emotion during her speech.

"Thank you so much to the Academy," she began her speech. "To the women in this category, Natalie [Portman], Isabelle [Huppert], Meryl [Streep], Ruth [Negga], you were all so extraordinary, and I look up to you, and I admire you more than I can put into words. It has been the greatest honor of all to stand along with you. To my mom and my dad

Emma, chosen for Best Actress for *La La Land* during the 89th Annual Academy Awards, February 2017

"I still have a lot of growing and learning and work to do. And this guy [her Oscar for *La La Land*] is a really beautiful symbol to continue on that journey and I'm so grateful for that."

and my brother, Spencer, and my soul sister, Chrissie, my whole family, I love you so much. Thank you for everything. To Doug Wald who stood by me all these years, Holly and Michelle and Craig and P.J. and Greta and Bob Cooper, thank you so much and I realize that a moment like this is a huge confluence of luck and opportunity, and so I want to thank Damian Chazelle for the opportunity to be part of a project that was so special and once in a lifetime. I'm so grateful to have been involved in this film, and thank you for your faith and your patience and such a wonderful experience. And Ryan Gosling, thank you for making me laugh and for always raising the bar and for being the greatest partner on this crazy adventure. To our whole crew, everyone that put their heart and souls into this film, I—I'm going to find you all individually, and I'm going to thank you. Along with my friends, who I love so much. I'm going to hug the hell out of you when the feeling re-enters my body. I still have a lot of growing and learning and work to do. And this guy is a really beautiful symbol to continue on that journey and I'm so grateful for that. So, thank you so much. Thank you."

Her next nomination for an Academy Award was for *The Favourite* in 2018, where she was recognized in the Best Supporting Actress category. The character of Abigail Masham also saw her nominated for a Golden Globe, a Screen Actors Guild Award, and a BAFTA.

In 2023, Emma won her second Academy Award for her role in *Poor Things*. She also took home a Golden Globe and a BAFTA for Best Actress.

Emma's speech at the Academy Awards showed her improv skills and personality, as she'd broken her dress moments before while dancing to friend Ryan Gosling's performance of "I'm Just Ken" from the film *Barbie*. She was out of breath as she took the award from Michelle Yeoh and best friend Jennifer Lawrence.

"Hoo boy, my dress is broken. I think it happened during 'I'm Just Ken.' I'm pretty sure. Oh, boy, this is really, this is really overwhelming. Sorry. My voice is also a little gone, whatever! The women on the stage, you are all incredible, and the women in this category: Sandra [Hüller],

Emma with Dave McCary after winning Best Actress in a Leading Role award for *Poor Things*, March 2024

Following: Scene from *Poor Things* where Emma played Bella Baxter, September 2023

CEMENTING CRITICAL ACCLAIM 137

"It's about a team that came together to make something greater than the sum of its parts. And that is the best part about making movies, is all of us together."

Annette [Bening], Carey [Mulligan], Lily [Gladstone], I share this with you. I am in awe of you, and it has been such an honor to do all of this together. I hope we get to keep doing more together. I don't know what I'm saying.

"Oh my God, I'm totally—OK, the other night I was panicking as you can kind of see—it happens a lot—that maybe something like this could happen. And Yorgos said to me, 'Please take yourself out of it,' and he was right, because it's not about me.

"It's about a team that came together to make something greater than the sum of its parts. And that is the best part about making movies, is all of us together. And I am so deeply honored to share this with every cast member, with every crew member, with every single person who poured their love and their care and their brilliance into the making of this film.

"And Yorgos, thank you for the gift of a lifetime in Bella Baxter. I am forever thankful for you. Thank you for inviting all of us to be members of this team. Thank you.

Emma accepting the Best Actress in a Leading Role award for *Poor Things* from close friend Jennifer Lawrence, also with Michelle Yeoh and Charlize Theron, during the 96th Annual Academy Awards, March 2024

"Oh, wait, I just—I know I have to wrap up, but I really just want to thank my family, my mom, my brother Spencer, my dad, my husband Dave. I love you so much. And most importantly, my daughter who's gonna be three in three days and has turned our lives technicolor. I love you bigger than the whole sky, my girl. So, thank you so much. Don't look at the back of my dress. Thank you."

During the 96th Annual Academy Awards show, Emma gives an acceptance speech, March 2024

CEMENTING CRITICAL ACCLAIM

Awards on Display

After winning the Oscar for Best Actress in *La La Land*, Emma went on *Late Night with Seth Meyers* to discuss the trophy.

"My mom has it," she said. "It felt a little strange." However, she did hold the prizes for two other achievements in her apartment at the time: "A Nickelodeon Kids' Choice Award—which is an orange blimp that is also a kaleidoscope—and my spelling bee trophy from the fourth grade." It was a moment deserving of a brag. "I got first place in the spelling bee."

Seth asked Emma if she remembered her winning word.

"I was trying to think about this for a little while. And what I remember it to be—I could be incorrect—was a compound word, which is 'microfinance.'"

She immediately challenged Seth to spell it. When he did it correctly, she joked, "And now I have to give you my trophy."

In 2023, after Emma won two Golden Globes, one for her performance in *Poor Things* and a second for producing the Best Motion Picture, she told *People* that she'd be keeping those awards with her.

"They might be on an airplane. Shaking. Scared. Unaware of where they are. All alone. Confused," she joked. "But I hope they're all right."

Emma with her mother, Krista Stone, at the 17th Annual Screen Actors Guild Awards in Los Angeles, January 2012

chapter 7

Emma's Fashion

"I think this is a wonderful time for women. I think the tide is turning, and there are so many brave, authentic, strong, and funny and vulnerable and exciting women in every industry right now."

—Emma quoted in *Glamour*

While Emma has always been interested in fashion, her dedication to style increased as she became a public figure. To keep things fresh and to stay current with the times, Emma has worked with celebrity fashion stylist Petra Flannery for decades. They met when the actor was eighteen years old and preparing to embark on the promotional tour for *The House Bunny* in 2008, and since that time, Petra has been the secret behind all Emma's looks, from interviews and awards shows to a day around town. Petra also looks after other Hollywood stars like Reese Witherspoon, Zoe Saldana, Faith Hill, and Claire Danes, but her relationship with Emma is a standout, attracting the attention of both Emma's fans and fashion enthusiasts worldwide.

Emma during Paris Fashion Week, March 2024

Emma with Rachel Goodwin and Petra Flannery at the Variety & WWD Host Second Annual StyleMakers Awards in West Hollywood, California, November 2016

"A lot of the times with Petra, when we do press for a particular film or show, we're together as a team discussing, and we get very inspired by the feeling of the film or the show. So that's really fun to sort of bring out the world of the story that I am promoting through the clothes that I wear."

In 2017, the *New York Times* published an article called "The Irresistible Style of Emma Stone," in which Petra spoke about her relationship with Emma and the actor's style. "She's very spirited when it comes to fashion," she said. "She's a very animated person, and my goal is to make the clothes complement all of that, whether it's through color, or a material that makes it unique, or an interesting design."

In *Harper's Bazaar*, Petra continued to gush about her client: "It is so amazing to work with Emma. She is so talented and creative. When it comes to dressing, she is definitely involved in the process, and she's very spirited when we're talking about fashion. Once we make decisions, she trusts me to follow through with the fine details. I really feel very lucky to have this relationship with her."

As with many of Emma's working relationships and friendships, the feeling is very much mutual. In 2023, *Vanity Fair*, Emma said about Petra, "She is the secret to anything I wear when I go somewhere, so it's all Petra. She really deserves all the credit. A lot of the times with Petra, when we do press for a particular film or show, we're together as a team discussing, and we get very inspired by the feeling of the film or the show. So that's really fun to sort of bring out the world of the story that I am promoting through the clothes that I wear."

Petra and Emma have worked together to create a rhythm for Emma's trendsetting looks. In that same *Vanity Fair* interview, Emma reflected on how desperately she needed fashion advice when she started in Hollywood.

"I was really into spray tan because I'm from Phoenix. I'm extremely pale, so I was really into tans and into heavy makeup, and I went through a couple of phases: trying to dress like Britney Spears circa 1999 to 2001, and then I kind of went into a mod phase that really did not work for me." Emma is not shy to admit, "I owe most things to Petra and her guidance."

That guidance brought Emma the honor of being named as *Glamour*'s "Style Icon of the Week" for April 21, 2014. The magazine fawned over Emma's looks, from daytime outings to evening celebrations, over the preceding years. The retrospective began with a look at the 2010 leather Pucci minidress that Emma wore to the MTV Video Music Awards. The following year, she wore a bright red "fringed lace-overlay cocktail dress" by Bottega Veneta to the MTV Movie Awards. At the 2012 Oscars, her hair was back to blonde from her signature red, and her dress was a Giambattista black gown. The *Amazing Spider-Man* premiere found Emma in a goth Gucci gown. And for *The Amazing Spider-Man 2*, she wore a leather Lanvin ball gown. *Glamour* especially loved this style, saying, "The detail is exquisite: the slick texture, the origami-esque folds, the sculptural silhouette, and the heavy metal belt. Sigh."

As Emma's name became more and more prominent, and award nominations and wins piled up, Petra leaned into a way that Emma's films could set the tone for awards shows and red-carpet displays. For example, when Emma was nominated for Best Actress in *La La Land*, she was seen at a party for *W Magazine* in a marigold floral Gucci dress that Petra called "the ultimate party dress." At the movie's premiere, Emma wore a crystal-encrusted sky-blue Prada dress, and at the Venice Film Festival, *La La Land*'s flirty Los Angeles theme continued with an Atelier Versace gown. *Vanity Fair* said that although Ryan Gosling wasn't with her at the 2016 Film Festival, "Stone's dress was so brilliant that it immediately rendered all other red-carpet occupants invisible—but we're sure that the reflection from Stone's shimmery ribbons reached him, wherever he was on the planet."

Emma posing at the 2010 MTV Video Music Awards in Los Angeles, California, September 2010

Opposite: Emma at *The Amazing Spider-Man* premiere at Le Grand Rex in Paris, France, June 2012

This concept of consciously bringing fashion together with film promotion is called "method dressing." In 2024, *Harper's Bazaar* explained how the popular merging of acting roles and outfit choices brought more creativity to couture. Method dressing isn't new, but in recent years, thanks in large part to Margot Robbie's *Barbie* promo tour (for which Margot often donned all-pink designer ensembles), it has expanded and taken on new life. And from there, the idea expanded into the audiences, where movie goers dressed up for the shows. Pink was everywhere, and method dressing exploded from clothing to accessories to makeup to footwear.

The same *Harper's Bazaar* article specifically mentioned Emma and the dress she wore to the 2024 BAFTAs in England. "While promoting her award-winning role in *Poor Things*, Emma Stone stepped out in a series of playful, exaggerated styles, in a nod to the vibrant colors and bold, big sleeves worn by her character in the film. Nowhere was this done more effectively than at the BAFTAs, where she picked up the award for Best Actress wearing [an] orange, multi-textured Louis Vuitton dress."

Emma at the 2024 EE BAFTA Film Awards in London, England, February 2024

Opposite: Emma at the premiere of *La La Land* during the 73rd Venice Film Festival, August 2016

EMMA'S FASHION

In fact, Emma's red-carpet wardrobe for *Poor Things* was considered a triumph for Petra Flannery. As Petra told *Harper's Bazaar* in a 2024 interview, "The approach was to play with color—a lot of color. We wanted to incorporate a nod to Bella Baxter so we focused on this, as well as bold shapes, exquisite fabrics, and a touch of sheer."

Method dressing, pulling from a project's costuming and theme, allows a base for the designer. But the overall look is greater than the dress. Emma's jewelry, shoes, hair, and makeup are vital as well.

Petra also spoke with *Harper's Bazaar* about the importance of jewelry. "The right jewelry is so important because it really helps take the look to another level," she explained. "The clothes should fit perfectly, and the jewelry should complement the style. The embellishment of jewelry really creates personality—you can make a minimalist look artful by adding a necklace or freshen up a suit with a big hoop."

Petra is careful in her selections when it comes to Emma's looks. She knows when to be playful or serious, vintage or modern, and she experiments with trends. If Emma's outfits are simple, her jewelry makes a bigger statement, and vice versa. And Petra makes sure that Emma is adorned appropriately for the occasion. For example, at the 2024 Oscars, Emma stood out in a white gold, sapphire, and diamond choker necklace. The Golden Globes found her in teardrop earrings. There were chunky studs for the *Poor Things* premiere. Fashion and jewelry can be used to blur the line between the celebrities and their work, augmenting fantasy and making a powerful statement.

While lavish, expensive jewels are expected for Hollywood celebrities, Emma sometimes also wears pieces from fan-friendly budget lines. At the 2024 AFI Awards luncheon, she stepped out in Brooklyn designer Aupen's Splash earrings. Even her engagement ring cost less than the average engagement ring—plus, it launched

---

Top left: Emma's bracelet detail at the 87th Annual Academy Awards, February 2015

Top right: Emma's accessory detail at the 19th Annual ELLE Women in Hollywood Celebration, October 2012

Bottom: Emma's necklace detail at the *Poor Things* premiere in New York City, New York, December 2023

Emma's shoe detail at the 2022 Met Gala in New York City, New York, May 2022

Opposite: World premiere of *The Amazing Spider-Man 2* in Central London, April 2014

new interest in rings with large pearls combined with diamonds. Emma's ring came from Catbird, a New York City jewelry store, and cost approximately $4,780, which is $7,829 below the national average for non-celebrities. That's also, of course, *far* below the price tag often ascribed to celebrities who spend much more on fancy gems, like Angelina Jolie, Blake Lively, and Beyoncé, who all have engagement rings appraised between $1 million and $5 million.

While the press often focuses on dresses and jewels, shoes are an important part of every outfit too. A list on *Footwear News* highlights some of Emma's best looks. For the Second Annual Academy Museum of Motion Pictures gala in 2022, she wore black velvet pumps. The 2022 Met Gala found the star in white pumps with a square toe, and the bejeweled ankle strap drew additional attention. In 2019, Emma wore ankle-star pumps with studded crystals covering the toe. Her shoes for *The Amazing Spider-Man* premiere in 2012 also boasted an embellished toe cap and see-through sides.

EMMA

In 2024, Emma stepped into an ongoing trend when she left the studio for the *Late Show with Stephen Colbert* wearing cherry-red loafers. Vogue felt the style was on-point, when they reported that the loafers were "from every minimalist celebrity's favorite luxury brand, The Row—with navy pleated trousers with a sleek, drainpipe silhouette. Stone completed the look with a simple beige crew-neck sweater and a delicate gold chain necklace. Emma's fashion formula here is straightforward: make the outfit clean and timeless but add a touch of red to keep things current." The shoes' price tag? $1,250.

In 2013, Emma had a long conversation with *Elle Canada* about her hair color. Originally a blonde, she dyed it red when she began to book Hollywood films. "Weirdly, I identify myself with red hair a bit more now, though. I felt like myself for a while when I first dyed it blonde, but the grass is always greener, you know? Or always redder or blonder on the other side." She finds the ongoing conversation and constant attention to her hair color funny, "But I've grown a little bit weary of the hair talk. I would keep it blonde because it's cheapest for me in terms of upkeep. But you know, studios are paying to change it, so it's a fantasy to have all these different hair colors."

Emma is also an ambassador for beauty giant Revlon. When she came on board in 2012, she was impressed by the company's philanthropic work supporting breast cancer research. She told *Yahoo*, "That is more what I think about when I think about that association—what they've done for women, and what they continue to do." Revlon supports many of the same charities that are near to Emma's heart, like Gilda's Club. "That's unbelievable to know you can have a hand in that. I got to do a PSA [screening test] with my mom, who is a breast cancer survivor. To be able to speak to women about early detection in a major way is really touching."

When she was asked to be a brand ambassador for Revlon, the charitable aspect resonated but the idea of promoting makeup didn't seem realistic, as Emma has often called her makeup routine "super slutty," because she bounces from product line to product line. When Emma told a reporter for *Elle Canada*, "I look down at my nails now and it looks like I was digging through a sandbox. I don't know what I get into, but by the look of my hands, it's pretty gross." But they wouldn't be gross for long—Revlon made Emma their face for a nail polish line.

The interviewer at *Elle Canada* remarked that she'd seen Emma's Revlon ads around town. "Oh, lord, sorry," Emma apologized. "I've seen them at drugstores and, for the most part, it's like 'Oh, my God, I need to go to a different aisle.' I feel totally freaked out because it takes you by surprise when you're going into, like, Walgreens and there's a picture of yourself. It's pretty terrifying."

Harper's Bazaar followed Emma around for a day in January 2024. The headline of the piece read, "Emma Stone Just Pulled Off Three Totally Fabulous, Utterly Distinct Looks in One Day" with the subheading: "The actor's versatile wardrobe is the gift that keeps on giving."

In the morning, fresh out of an interview with *Good Morning America*, Emma wore a "business casual ensemble" by Louis Vuitton, including a powder-blue, button-up shirt paired with a camel-colored midi skirt. The weather was chilly, so she wore a double-breasted beige coat with rounded lapels and light brown, knee-high suede boots. Earrings from Tiffany & Co completed the look.

That evening, Emma walked into the *Late Show with Stephen Colbert* wearing a black tweed blazer by Louis Vuitton. Instead of

Emma in New York City, New York, January 2024

Emma at the UK film premiere of *The Favourite* during the 62nd London Film Festival, October 2018

Opposite top left: Emma at the 91st Annual Academy Awards in Hollywood, California, February 2019

Opposite top right: Emma during Paris Fashion Week, March 2023

Opposite bottom: Emma at the 75th Venice Film Festival, August 2018

buttoning the jacket, she chose to hook a satin scarf through the jacket, which was an alternative by the designer. Her skirt was also Louis Vuitton. She wore simple black pumps and a gold chain link necklace and knot rings from Tiffany & Co.

It was when Emma left the show that she donned those red loafers that were so "on trend." *Harper's Bazaar* swooned at Emma's fashion savvy and yet casual look: "At the end of the day, the *Easy A* star was spotted on the streets of Manhattan in a slate-colored sweater with ribbed hems, which she paired with navy slacks and bright red loafers— championing this year's burgeoning candy-apple red trend. To round out the look, Stone wore diamond stud earrings and kept her gold streak going with a pair of stacked golden necklaces. What a hat trick, Emma."

Stylist Petra says that she and Emma have such great connection that they share inside jokes. As Petra revealed during an interview with *British Vogue* in 2017, "We find humor in vintage times. We love to speak as if we are from the Forties. It's a take on Katharine Hepburn and Cary Grant's transatlantic accents."

In a final comment for the *New York Times* in 2017, Petra had this to say about Emma Stone: "It's true designers love her, but also Emma appreciates fashion from an artist's point of view. Style is innate. It's in her bones."

Emma is also never shy to repurpose a dress. She wore a Louis Vuitton white dress to the 2022 Met Gala, which she also wore at her wedding. *Brides* said, "Rewearing the dress is definitely a statement on sustainability, and we are here for it. We are also in love with the sheer illusion straps and feather adorned hem that gives the number a modern flapper vibe. We also love how the beautiful Louis Vuitton dress looks paired with her unique pearl engagement ring." And of course, "While we would have loved to see how Stone styled the look on her wedding day, we are happy to get a taste of it with her sweet style at the Met Gala, too."

Emma at the 2022 Met Gala at the Metropolitan Museum of Art in New York City, New York, May 2022

Emma poses for a Louis Vuitton presentation held at Palazzo Borromeo in Isola Bella, Italy, May 2023

The Brand Ambassador Bonus

In 2012, Emma, alongside Olivia Wilde, became a brand ambassador for Revlon. Alan T. Ennis, Revlon's President and Chief Executive Officer, announced the deal, saying, "We are absolutely thrilled to welcome Emma and Olivia into the Revlon family. These remarkably talented actresses personify the Revlon woman—glamorous, confident, and bold. Together, they will help us build meaningful connections with new consumers and strengthen our relationship with existing fans of our brand. Each has a unique style, personality, and look that appeals to a broad range of women."

For Emma, this didn't only mean her face on ads and campaigns for make-up and nail polish, but also support for the business's philanthropic efforts. Before Emma came on board, Revlon had already given more than $65 million to women's cancer research.

These ambassador deals bring attention to the product and the causes the company supports, but they're also incredibly lucrative for the ambassadors. Some of the highest paid brand ambassadors include soccer stars Cristiano Ronaldo, who earned $1 billion for his lifetime deal with Nike, and David Beckham, who was paid $160 million by Adidas. Beyoncé's price tag was $50 million for her work with Pepsi.

When Emma Stone took on her second brand deal, becoming an ambassador for Louis Vuitton, it's estimated that her two-year contract earned her between $6 and $10 million. *Page Six* reported that the team at Louis Vuitton had actively pursued Emma for two years for a deal that would put her in "glossy TV and print ads worldwide" in addition to a commitment to "wear their high-end gowns on the red carpet."

In 2023, Emma's relationship with Louis Vuitton was renewed. During COVID, creative director Nicolas Ghesquière reflected on changes he wanted to make for the upcoming Fall/Winter 2023 line. He bandied around the question, "What is French style?"

Emma was at Paris's world acclaimed Fashion Week to debut the line. *Women's Wear Daily* reported, "Emma Stone arrived at Louis Vuitton's fall 2023 runway show during Paris Fashion Week on Monday, taking a colorful approach to power dressing. To support the brand in unveiling its latest runway collection, the actress wore a blue suit with blood-orange pinstripes. Underneath the suit she wore a light-blue button-up shirt. She coordinated the look with a pair of pointy-toe ballet-style heels. She topped off the ensemble by accessorizing with a black top-handle handbag. Stone's full look was from Louis Vuitton."

The dress that Emma wore to the 2024 Oscars was also by Louis Vuitton. When the zipper broke just before she accepted her award for *Poor Things*, Emma responded with her classic humor, saying, "The other night I was panicking, as you can kind of see happens a lot, that maybe something like this could happen."

Afterward, Emma quick-changed into a sparkly silver Louis Vuitton gown and made her way to the Vanity Fair Oscars Party. Just another day for a brand ambassador.

Emma models for a UK Louis Vuitton magazine advertisement

EMMA'S FASHION 165

chapter 8

Impact, Influence, and Legacy

"I won't make a bucket list because I'm so afraid that I'll die and then people will find my bucket list and be like, 'Oh, she didn't get to do that . . .' There is stuff that I'd like to do or experience, but nothing that would crush me if it didn't happen."

—Emma talking to Cameron Crowe for *Interview Magazine* in 2012

Emma is known not just for her films and awards, her fashion, and her down-to-earth humor. She is also recognized as a face for important charitable causes.

One of her most profound steps toward raising awareness for philanthropic causes close to her heart was in response to the growing

---

Emma enjoying the CFDA/Vogue Fashion Fund Show and Tea in Los Angeles, California, October 2016

intrusion of the paparazzi when she was dating Andrew Garfield. Since cameras followed them everywhere, the duo decided to use their power for good. In 2012, they were spotted on the street, holding handmade signs. Emma's read: "We just found out that there were paparazzi outside the restaurant we were eating in. So . . . why not take this"—she'd drawn an arrow to Andrew, who held the rest of the message—"opportunity to bring attention to organizations that need and deserve it." The sign included links to the Rise Alliance for Children (formerly the WWO) and Gilda's Club, and closed with a cheeky, "Have a great day!"

Emma's relationship with Gilda's Club New York City began after her mom was diagnosed with triple-negative breast cancer in 2008. Emma was only nineteen at the time and between shooting movies, but rushed to her mother's side as Krista Stone endured a double mastectomy and a year and a half of chemotherapy treatments.

Since then, Emma has given her time and resources to multiple cancer awareness charities like Gilda's Club NYC, for whom she acts as ambassador. Gilda's Club was named for comedian Gilda Radner, famous for the groundbreaking roles she played on *Saturday Night Live*, who passed away from ovarian cancer in 1989. The non-profit opened its doors in 1995 to provide support, resources, and community for patients and their families. In 2000, the group expanded to Gilda's Club Worldwide and in 2021 rebranded as the Red Door Community.

At the 2014 Entertainment Industry Foundation's Revlon Run/Walk, Emma, a Revlon ambassador, said, "As an actor, I end up talking about movies that I'm a part of, which is great, but to be able to talk about something that can really make some fundamental change in terms of—I can't cure cancer, or treat it—but the fact that I can be part of something that really is able to give back in such a major way is a big honor."

Other charities that Emma has supported include the American Association for Cancer Research, American Civil Liberties Union, Boys & Girls Clubs of America, Los Angeles LGBT Center, Stand Up to Cancer, and the charity on the sign she shared with Andrew Garfield, the Rise Alliance for Children.

Emma attending the Women Working & Living with Cancer Annual Benefit in New York City, New York, May 2013

IMPACT, INFLUENCE, AND LEGACY

"As an actor, I end up talking about movies that I'm a part of, which is great, but to be able to talk about something that can really make some fundamental change in terms of—I can't cure cancer, or treat it—but the fact that I can be part of something that really is able to give back in such a major way is a big honor."

A ROLE MODEL FOR HONESTY

From the very beginning of her Hollywood story, Emma has been vocal about her feelings of panic, fear and anxiety, and coping techniques. In an interview with NPR in 2024, Emma recounted how she had her first panic attack at age seven. When reporter Terry Gross asked about that early experience, Emma was very candid. "I mean, people have different experiences of panic attacks. I know a lot of people feel like they're dying or that the walls are closing in on them. And I certainly have had those types of panic attacks," she explained. "I've had probably hundreds throughout my life. So, my very first one, when I was seven—I was at a friend's house, and all of a sudden, I was just sitting in her room, and I had this deep knowing that the house was on fire. I believed the house was on fire, despite all evidence to the contrary. . . . my chest just started tightening, and I was like, 'We have to get out of the house. The house is burning down. The house is burning down.'

"And I ended up calling my mom, who didn't understand what was going on and confirmed there wasn't a fire but came to pick me up. And then it just—it kept going. I just kept having panic attacks relatively frequently. And I started in therapy, I think, around age eight because it was getting really hard for me to leave the house to go to school. I sort of lived in fear of these panic attacks."

She attributed those feelings to separation anxiety from her mom and the terror that if she wasn't around, something bad might happen. Knowing the feelings were irrational didn't help her cope with them at the time. Getting help was important.

"And it's a tough one to unpack until you have sort of the tools to do it or the understanding of it through therapy, which—I was so grateful that, you know—I didn't want to go to therapy," she said on NPR. "But I found it really, really life-changing."

At the age of nine, she wrote a book for herself titled *I Am Bigger Than My Anxiety*. Although Emma's not an artist, she drew the pictures to go with the text. She told Terry Gross, "But the idea was externalizing the anxiety as this little green monster that lives on your shoulder. And the more you listen to this, the bigger this monster grows, the

Emma at the 5th Biennial Stand Up To Cancer event at the Walt Disney Concert Hall in Los Angeles, California, September 2016

IMPACT, INFLUENCE, AND LEGACY

"I'm drawn much more to comedy, or now, dark comedy. I felt like every reaction in my body is permitted. All of my big feelings are productive."

more power it has. But as you feel the fear and kind of do it anyway and continue to push through, the monster kind of shrinks and shrinks and shrinks. And I think that externalization, that making it that it's not you—it's a part of you, but it's not you—was very helpful."

Acting helped too. "And I'm drawn much more to comedy, or now, dark comedy. I felt like every reaction in my body is permitted. All of my big feelings are productive," she said. "And presence is required, so it's like a meditation because anxiety lives solely in the past or the future—you know, either future tripping or past tripping—you know, things you can't control on either side. And acting requires you to be so present, to listen, to be looking at the other person, to be living in the experience and living in your body. And that was the huge gift of it to me and remains the huge gift of it to me to this day."

Her parents' support, and her mother taking her to Los Angeles, were instrumental in facing her fears and managing her anxiety. Even as she struggled to figure out what was true and what was false information inside her, Emma found her place by channeling characters. Through acting, be it in the theater or in a film, she found a place between feeling nervous and being safe.

Scene from Yorgos Lanthimos's *Poor Things* starring Emma as Bella Baxter, 2023

IMPACT, INFLUENCE, AND LEGACY 173

"The high stakes is that you're either in front of an audience or you're—you know, this is being committed to film and will eventually last forever," she continued on NPR. "But the low stakes is that you're acting, you're storytelling. Nobody's going to die, and you're not saving any lives. You know, they're not on the operating table. So that feeling of, you know, fear mixed with joy is—that's my favorite combination."

At the end of the NPR interview, Emma talked about her commitment to therapy. When Terry asked about how she manages conflicting feelings, Emma replied, "Terry, the story of my life. . . . this is what I talk about in therapy on a weekly basis."

Emma's speech at the Academy Awards for *Poor Things* reflected her daily struggle. When her dress zipper broke, she recounted a bit of advice that director Yorgos Lanthimos had told her: "Yorgos said to me, 'Please take yourself out of it,' and he was right, because it's not about me."

That message from Yorgos was key to her portrayal of Bella in *Poor Things*. In an interview with *Variety* in 2024, Emma said that one of the things she really resonated with the character was "the idea of not living with that self-judgment or shame, as you say, or the social contracts that you make as a child growing up. And part of the nature of anxiety is that

"I believe the people who have anxiety and depression are very, very sensitive and very, very smart. Because the world is hard and scary and there's a lot that goes on and if you're very attuned to it, it can be crippling. But if you don't let it cripple you and use it for something productive, it's like a superpower."

you're always watching yourself. In some ways—this is horrible to say—it's a very selfish condition to have. Not to insult other people with anxiety—I still have it—but it's because you're thinking about yourself a lot. You're thinking about, 'What's going to happen to me? What have I said? What have I done?' Whereas Bella's way of approaching the world, it's just about experience. It's just about how she feels about things."

Emma's open sharing of the ways in which she manages anxiety resonates with her fans. One of her techniques is to write down the things that worry her. In a 2020 video for the Child Mind Institute, she gave some advice to those who feel anxiety. "I just write and write and write. I don't think about it, I don't read it back, and I usually do this before bed so [these worries or anxieties] don't interfere with my sleep. I find it's really helpful for me to just get it all out on paper." She has also said that she meditates, blasts music, exercises, and dances. Physical activity can be helpful. When she dances, Emma "gets very silly and very loose."

Earlier, in 2018, Emma said in another interview for the Child Mind Institute, where she serves on the board, "I believe the people who have anxiety and depression are very, very sensitive and very, very smart. Because the world is hard and scary and there's a lot that goes on and if you're very attuned to it, it can be crippling. But if you don't let it cripple you and use it for something productive, it's like a superpower."

When she filmed a video for the Institute's "Getting Better Together" campaign, she summed up her feelings by saying, "Everybody struggles with a little bit of sadness, or a little bit of worry, or fear around the idea of change in general . . . everybody has some of those feelings inside whether they're saying it or not. I just want you to know, you're very normal . . . keep talking about how you feel and share it with people you feel safe with. We're gonna be okay."

While for many celebrities, social media is a way of promoting their newest projects and connecting to fans, Emma remains on the sidelines. Her shunning of social media stems from understanding her own anxiety and the associated triggers.

In 2018, *Elle* had Emma's best friend Jennifer Lawrence interview Emma. Jennifer asked about Emma's social media and the star replied, "I think it wouldn't be a positive thing for me. If people can handle that sort of output and input in the social media sphere, power to them."

A few years earlier, in 2014, Emma was on a panel with Tilda Swinton, Patricia Arquette, and Laura Dern for *The Los Angeles Times* and EPIX's TV series *Hollywood Sessions*. She explained why she shuns social media, saying that "It's that need to be liked, that need to be seen, that need to be validated, in a way, through no one that you know. And so people ask the question about fame, or what it feels like, and it seems like everybody knows what that feels like. It seems like everyone's cultivating their lives on Instagram or on different forms of social media, and what pictures looks best of their day."

It's not that she doesn't look at social media. Emma just doesn't have the desire to have her own account anymore. Her anxiety would result in fear based on world events, and then, when she said something off, she'd be terrified by the reactions. There's also fear of that old pressure of "keeping up with the Joneses."

Emma participating in a Q&A ahead of a UK screening of *Poor Things*, 2023

EMMA

"Not everything comes **together** in the best way ever, every day. It just doesn't. Even when your **dream** you set out for comes true, it's not always perfect. . . . That's not the **reality** of **life.**"

In 2016, she elaborated on her thoughts in an *Elle* interview. "That's why it makes me so crazy to look at social media. When you see people like, 'This is the best life ever! I couldn't be happier.' You're like, 'Shut up, that is not true.' Not everything comes together in the best way ever, every day. It just doesn't. Even when your dream you set out for comes true, it's not always perfect. . . . That's not the reality of life."

Emma knew early on that social media wouldn't be healthy for her, but she quickly discovered that quitting social meant also meant giving up her favorite game. In 2012, she already realized she had an issue with social media when she had to leave Facebook in order to get rid of her addiction. As she told Jimmy Fallon, "I had to delete Facebook because I was addicted to *Farmville*. . . . It's a fake farm, but it doesn't feel fake, Jimmy. I ended up leaving dinners to harvest . . . real dinners!"

When talking to the *Hollywood Reporter* in 2024, she was asked, yet again, why she is not on social media. Emma replied, "I can't do it. I'm not built for it. There's already enough going on in my head. I, I would just panic and melt down and overthink everything I said . . . I should never be adding anything that's going to make me freak out. You know what I mean? And it feels like that would make me freak out."

Emma's fans adore her for her acting and praise the awards she earns, but beyond all that, the public resonates with her honesty, the truth she speaks, her commitment to charitable causes, and the way she addresses mental health.

At a Q and A in London for *Poor Things*, a fan took the microphone and said, "Everything you create is pure and honest . . . Your heart is your confidence, your energy, your wicked strength, your advocacy for mental health awareness. Growing up I was one of the few artistic kids in school. I felt lonely and unable to make friends. During recess, I would sneak inside the computer room to watch your old *SNL* sketches. . . . the safety you brought me during those years."

His comment was enough to get Emma out of her chair. She rushed to the floor and hugged her fan.

Emma's Quick Questions

In 2016, *Vogue* peppered Emma with seventy-three questions, giving her only a short time to think about the answers. The spontaneous answers gave insight into who she is, and how she sees the world.

To start things off, she was pressed to answer the difference between living in New York and Los Angeles. When the reporter asked, "What's the best thing about being in Los Angeles?" Emma replied, "The weather and my friends." And the best thing about New York City? "The plays."

The interviewer continued with another rapid-fire question: "What historical figure would you love to have coffee with?" Her answer wasn't surprising, seeing as she both works with the comedian's charity and is also a fan of *SNL*. Emma replied easily, "Gilda Radner."

When asked, "What have you learned about being an actress?" Emma answered, "A lot of things. I think mostly that if you take care of yourself and you pay attention, the better you'll be." And which movies inspired her? "*The Jerk*, *Annie Hall*, *Hocus Pocus*, and *Beetlejuice*."

Emma's favorite foods are "French fries and Brussels sprouts, not necessarily at the same time." And her least favorite, "Beets and anything with mayo."

IMPACT, INFLUENCE, AND LEGACY

As a prolific reader, Emma said that *Raise High the Roof Beam, Carpenters* by J. D. Salinger is her favorite book and noted that she always travels with a book in her bag.

The first thing she did the morning of the interview was meditate, which for years she has touted as a way to help manage her anxiety.

Her playful spirit came out in the way she answered the question of how she'd describe herself in three words. Emma didn't miss a beat: "Probably 'very effing cool.'"

She revealed that her favorite superhero is Spider-Man, and while that might not be a surprise, she wowed the interviewer with her "secret talent": Emma can type 100 words a minute.

As the interview wrapped up, the reporter had an important question. "Nicknames?"

Emma Stone didn't need to think about her answer. She said, "People mostly call me Em and my real name is Emily. Emma is actually short for that, so just please call me Emily."

Emma at *The Favourite* press conference at the Venice Film Festival, August 2017

IMPACT, INFLUENCE, AND LEGACY

The *Conclusion* Next Chapter

"My favorite bit of wisdom is that if you knew everyone's story, you would love them. You can't really hate anyone if you know everything that happened to them between their birth and now, why they became the way they became, why they have walls up or down. If you truly know someone, you'd get it."

— Emma quoted in *Glamour*

Now, with her name engraved on awards, and "Emma Stone" shining from theater marquees, Emma Stone would like to be called Emily. There are a long line of actors who have asked fans to call them by another name. Jodi Foster's birth name is Alicia. Whoopi Goldberg is Caryn Elaine Johnson. Natalie Portman was born Neta-Lee Hershlag, and like Emma, her friends and family call her by her given name. Michael Keaton, also like Emma, had to take on a new name because his real name, Michael Douglas, was already attached to another actor in the Screen Actors Guild.

Emma at the 77th Annual Cannes Film Festival in Cannes, France, on May 18, 2024

Following: Emma at the 77th Annual Cannes Film Festival in Cannes, France, on May 17, 2024

"My favorite bit of wisdom is that if you knew everyone's story, you would love them."

When Emma Stone's *The Curse* costar, Nathan Fielder, told the *Hollywood Reporter* in April 2024, "Her name's Emily, but she goes by Emma professionally. So, when there's people that don't know her, I end up saying Emma. But I'm going to just say 'Emily' from here on." That interview opened the door for Emma Stone to introduce the greater public to her real name.

In that same *Hollywood Reporter* interview, she was asked, "If some fan came up to you and said, 'Can I take a selfie, Emily?' would you be like, 'It's Emma.'"

Emma immediately replied, "No. That would be so nice. I would like to be Emily."

She was already known as Emily, or sometimes Em, on movie sets. Sitting down with director Yorgos Lanthimos for *Variety*, Yorgos seemed momentarily confused about what to call the actor. He was talking about Emma's interview process for *The Favourite*, their first movie together, when he said, "So there's always this thing where casting directors or agents are asking, 'Is this an offer?' And I always go, 'Well, I need us to meet first.' How am I going to offer a part if I don't speak to the person, see how we get along? So, we met and we got along really well. And, yeah, I guess my only question, because I'm not a native Anglophone, was about the accent. And so, we just did some . . ." He wasn't quite sure what to call the actor sitting beside him: "Emily, Emma, what am I calling you here?"'

Emma replied, "My name's Emily. Can you just call me Emily?"

From 2024 onward, there will be a lot more coming from the actor, producer, and now mother. *Kinds of Kindness* follows *Poor Things* with director Yorgos Lanthimos at the helm. *Fantasmas* has an episode with Emma. She's starring in and producing both *Bugonia* (with Yorgos Lanthimos directing) and *Cruella 2*. Emma continues to produce, alongside her husband, David McCary, through their company Fruit Tree. How will she be referred to in the credits for upcoming shows? Will awards be engraved to Emily instead of Emma? It's unclear how, or when, the public will respond to the name change, but already a shift is occurring. While at the 2024 Cannes Film Festival, promoting *Kinds of Kindness*, a reporter in the audience referred to her as "Emily."

Emma was delighted, joyfully exclaiming, "That's my name!"

Emma with director Yorgos Lanthimos and actor Willem Dafoe at the *Kinds of Kindness* press conference ahead of the 77th annual Cannes Film Festival at Palais des Festivals in Cannes, France, on May 18, 2024

A scene from *The Favourite* where Emma plays the role of Abigail, September 2018

Filmography

FILM

Acting

2007
Superbad (Role: Jules)

2008
The Rocker (Role: Amelia Stone)
The House Bunny (Role: Natalie Sandler)

2009
Ghosts of Girlfriends Past (Role: Allison Vandermeersh)
Paper Man (Role: Abby)
Zombieland (Role: Wichita / Krista)

2010
Marmaduke (Role: Mazie [voice])
Easy A   (Role: Olive Penderghast)

2011
Friends with Benefits (Role: Kayla)
Crazy, Stupid, Love (Role: Hannah Weaver)
The Help (Role: Eugenia "Skeeter" Phelan)

2012
The Amazing Spider-Man (Role: Gwen Stacy)

2013
Gangster Squad (Role: Grace Faraday)
Movie 43 (Role: Veronica)
The Croods (Role: Eep Crood [voice])

2014
The Amazing Spider-Man 2 (Role: Gwen Stacy)
Magic in the Moonlight (Role: Sophie Baker)
Birdman or (The Unexpected Virtue of Ignorance) (Role: Sam Thomson)
The Interview (Role: Herself [cameo])

2015
Aloha (Role: Allison Ng)
Irrational Man (Role: Jill Pollard)

2016
Popstar: Never Stop Never Stopping (Role: Claudia Cantrell [uncredited cameo])
La La Land (Role: Mia Dolan)

2017
Battle of the Sexes (Role: Billie Jean King)

2018
The Favourite (Role: Abigail Masham)

2019
Zombieland: Double Tap (Role: Wichita / Krista)

2020
The Croods: A New Age (Role: Eep Crood [voice])

2021
Cruella (Role: Estella / Cruella de Vil also executive producer)

2022
Bleat (short film) (Role: Woman)

2023
Poor Things (Role: Bella Baxter; also producer)

2024
Kinds of Kindness (Roles: Rita / Liz / Emily)

Producing

2022
When You Finish Saving the World

2023
Problemista
Producer

2024
I Saw the TV Glow
A Real Pain

TELEVISION

Acting

2004
The New Partridge Family (Role: Laurie Partridge)

2005
Medium (Role: Cynthia McCallister; episode: "Sweet Dreams")

2006
The Suite Life of Zack and Cody (Role: Ivana Tipton [voice]; episode: "Crushed"; credited as Emily Stone)
Malcolm in the Middle (Role: Diane; episode: "Lois Strikes Back")
Lucky Louie (Role: Shannon; episode: "Get Out")

2007
Drive (Role: Violet Trimble)

2010–2023
Saturday Night Live (Roles: Herself [host] and various characters; 8 episodes [host of 5 episodes])

2011
Robot Chicken (Roles: Various voices; 2 episodes)

2012

30 Rock (Role: Herself; episode: "The Ballad of Kenneth Parcell")
iCarly (Role: Heather, episode: "iFind Spencer Friends")

2016

Maya & Marty (Role: Herself; episode: "Sean Hayes, Steve Martin, Kelly Ripa & Emma Stone")

2018

Maniac (Role: Annie Landsberg; also executive producer)

2023–2024

The Curse (Role: Whitney Siegel; also executive producer)

2024

Fantasmas (Role: Genevieve; episode: "The Void"; guest star and executive producer)

Select Awards and Nominations

ACADEMY AWARDS

2015: Best Supporting Actress, *Birdman or (The Unexpected Virtue of Ignorance)* (Nominated)
2017: Best Actress, *La La Land* (Won)
2019: Best Supporting Actress, *The Favourite* (Nominated)
2024: Best Actress, *Poor Things* (Won)
*In 2024, *Poor Things* was also nominated for Best Picture

BAFTA AWARDS

2011: BAFTA Rising Star Award (Nominated)
2015: Best Actress in a Supporting Role, *Birdman or (The Unexpected Virtue of Ignorance)* (Nominated)
2017: Best Actress in a Leading Role, *La La Land* (Won)
2019: Best Actress in a Supporting Role, *The Favourite* (Nominated)
*In 2024, *Poor Things* was also nominated for Best Film and Outstanding British Film

GOLDEN GLOBE AWARDS

2011: Best Actress in a Motion Picture – Musical or Comedy, *Easy A* (Nominated)
2015: Best Supporting Actress – Motion Picture, *Birdman or (The Unexpected Virtue of Ignorance)* (Nominated)
2017: Best Actress in a Motion Picture – Musical or Comedy, *La La Land* (Won)
2018: Best Actress in a Motion Picture – Musical or Comedy, *Battle of the Sexes* (Nominated)
2019: Best Supporting Actress – Motion Picture, *The Favourite* (Nominated)

2022: Best Actress in a Motion Picture – Musical or Comedy, *Cruella* (Nominated)

2024: Best Actress in a Motion Picture – Musical or Comedy, *Poor Things* (Won)

2024: Best Actress in a Television Series – Drama, *The Curse* (Nominated)

SCREEN ACTORS GUILD AWARDS

2012: Outstanding Performance by a Cast in a Motion Picture, *The Help* (Won)

2015: Outstanding Performance by a Cast in a Motion Picture, *Birdman or (The Unexpected Virtue of Ignorance)* (Won)

2015: Outstanding Performance by a Female Actor in a Supporting Role, *Birdman or (The Unexpected Virtue of Ignorance)* (Nominated)

2017: Outstanding Performance by a Female Actor in a Leading Role, *La La Land* (Won)

2019: Outstanding Performance by a Female Actor in a Miniseries or Television Movie, *Maniac* (Nominated)

2019: Outstanding Performance by a Female Actor in a Supporting Role, *The Favourite* (Nominated)

2024: Outstanding Performance by a Female Actor in a Leading Role, *Poor Things* (Nominated)

VENICE FILM FESTIVAL

2016: Volpi Cup for Best Actress, *La La Land* (Won)

CRITICS' CHOICE AWARDS

2012: Best Acting Ensemble, *The Help* (Won)

2015: Best Acting Ensemble, *Birdman or (The Unexpected Virtue of Ignorance)* (Won)

2015: Best Supporting Actress, *Birdman or (The Unexpected Virtue of Ignorance)* (Nominated)

2017: Best Actress, *La La Land* (Nominated)

2018: Best Actress in a Comedy Movie, *Battle of the Sexes* (Nominated)

2019: Best Acting Ensemble, *The Favourite* (Won)

2019: Best Supporting Actress, *The Favourite* (Nominated)

2024: Best Movie, *Poor Things* (Nominated)
2024: Best Actress, *Poor Things* (Won)

INDEPENDENT SPIRIT AWARDS
2015: Best Supporting Female, *Birdman or (The Unexpected Virtue of Ignorance)* (Nominated)

PRODUCERS GUILD AWARDS
2019: Outstanding Producer of Limited Series Television, *Maniac* (Nominated)
2024: Outstanding Producer of Theatrical Motion Pictures, *Poor Things* (Nominated)

Emma accepts Best Actress for *La La Land* at the 89th Annual Academy Awards, February 2017

Sources

Abramovitch, Seth. "Nathan Fielder and Emma Stone Take a Ride on the Wild Side as TV's Cringiest Couple." *The Hollywood Reporter*, 25 Apr. 2024, www.hollywoodreporter.com/tv/tv-features/emma-stone-nathan-fielder-interview-the-curse-1235879506/.

Arnold, Ben. "Emma Stone Reveals the Hilariously Bad Reason She Stopped Using Her Real Name." Yahoo! Movies, 13 Nov. 2018, uk.movies.yahoo.com/movies/emma-stone-reveals-hilariously-bad-reason-stopped-using-real-name-094537813.html?guce_referrer=aHR0cHM6Ly9lbi53aWtpcGVkaWEub3JnLw&guce_referrer_sig=AQAAADAa8f_vl1ypr1RCqm0Sx5x_TQkk-lovOPHa5i3q9qcDlZlCplgB1Fiv3-f8JBZE1ulcyEZzIAA_PlUhXjL1l3V_SpIn15KL9BgRC9vEHUIFqH3qw478nVA3RPYtJqnWLNGX7nZf7vLK-CvvEeoVSCJhjmTPctlz5TcDZfaVeQkaJj&guccounter=2.

Barna, Ben. "'Zombieland's' Emma Stone Dreams of SNL and Mexican Food." *BlackBook*, 2 Oct. 2009, web.archive.org/web/20111022221855/www.blackbookmag.com/article/zombielands-emma-stone-dreams-of-snl-and-mexican-food/11382.

Brockington, Ariana. "Emma Stone Clarifies Whether She Goes by Emma or Emily after Cannes Film Festival Confusion." Today.com, 20 June 2024, www.today.com/popculture/news/emma-stone-use-real-name-emily-rcna149470.

Child Mind Institute. "How #wethriveinside with Actor Emma Stone." Facebook, 1 May 2020, www.facebook.com/ChildMindInstitute/videos/675688103267780/.

Crowe, Cameron. "Emma Stone on Coronado." Coronado Visitor Center, 7 Aug. 2020, coronadovisitorcenter.com/emma-stone-on-coronado/.

Emma at the premiere of *The Amazing Spider-Man 2* at Odeon Leicester Square in London, April 2014

Diehl, Jessica, et al. "Emma Stone: Hollywood Is Her Oyster." *Vanity Fair*, 31 Jan. 2015, web.archive.org/web/20160312131935/www.vanityfair.com/news/2011/08/emma-stone-201108.

"Emma Stone on La La Land, Robert De Niro, and Sucking Her Thumb Until 11 | Screen Tests | W Magazine." YouTube, W Magazine, 3 Jan. 2017, www.youtube.com/watch?v=i56ag3hXW3k.

"Emma Stone Wants You to Call Her 'Emily.'" *Vanity Fair*, 27 Apr. 2024, www.vanityfair.com/hollywood/story/emma-stone-wants-you-to-call-her-emily.

Fisher, Luchina. "Emma Stone Has History of Panic Attacks." ABC News, 21 June 2012, abcnews.go.com/blogs/entertainment/2012/06/emma-stone-has-history-of-panic-attacks/.

Hirschberg, Lynn. "Emma Stone Was Nervous About Singing in *La La Land*, But Not About Admitting That She Sucks Her Thumb." *W Magazine*, 3 Jan. 2017, www.wmagazine.com/story/emma-stone-was-nervous-about-singing-in-la-la-land.

Hudson, Kathryn. "Emma Stone: The Elle Canada Interview: Elle Canada Magazine: Beauty, Fashion and Lifestyle Trends & Celebrity News." *ELLE Canada Magazine* , 8 Apr. 2013, www.ellecanada.com/culture/celebrity/emma-stone-the-elle-canada-interview.

IMDb. "Emma Stone: Stars' Early Parts." Facebook, 30 Nov. 2018, www.facebook.com/imdb/videos/2116103665113437/.

Jason Gay, Mert Alas, and Marcus Piggott. "Emma Stone Takes the Biggest Leap of Her Career with La La Land." *Vogue*, 14 Oct. 2016, www.vogue.com/article/emma-stone-november-cover-la-la-land-movie-ryan-gosling.

Mancuso, Vinnie. "Emma Stone on the Art of Unlearning Everything." Backstage, 24 Jan. 2024, www.backstage.com/magazine/article/emma-stone-poor-things-interview-photos-76833.

Miller, Mike. "Oscars 2017: Emma Stone Journey to Stardom." People.com, 27 Feb. 2017, people.com/celebrity/how-emma-stone-left-home-at-14-completed-project-hollywood-and-won-her-first-oscar/.

Mzezewa, Tariro. "Emma Stone Wants You to Call Her 'Emily.'" *The Cut*, 26 Apr. 2024, www.thecut.com/article/emma-stone-real-name.html.

"Oscars Round Table: Emma Stone on Social Media." *Los Angeles Times*, 7 Dec. 2014, www.latimes.com/82216454-132.html.

Picciotti, Tyler. "Emma Stone Is Now a Two-Time Oscar Winner for Best Actress." Biography.com, 10 Mar. 2024, www.biography.com/actors/emma-stone.

Rice, Alex. "Emma Stone Uses Acting to 'Understand Human Behavior.'" Perth Film School, 29 Oct. 2015, perthfilmschool.com.au/emma-stone-uses-acting-to-understand-human-behavior/.

Spencer, Amy. "Emma Stone: The Cool Girl." *Glamour*, 29 Mar. 2011, www.glamour.com/story/emma-stone-the-cool-girl.

Staff, Extra. "Emma Stone Finds It Hard Not to Be Funny." Extra, 17 Jan. 2013, extratv.com/2013/01/17/emma-stone-finds-it-hard-not-to-be-funny/.

Wilner, Norman. "Q&A: Emma Stone." *NOW Magazine*, 27 July 2011, web.archive.org/web/20120620013944/www.nowtoronto.com/daily/movies/story.cfm?content=181989.

Wolfe, Alexandra. "Emma Stone: Hollywood Is Her Oyster." *Vanity Fair*, 21 June 2011, www.vanityfair.com/news/2011/08/emma-stone-201108.

Photo Credits

p. 2 Gareth Cattermole/Getty Images Entertainment/Getty Images Europe. **p. 4** Francois G. Durand/WireImage/Getty Images Entertainment/Getty Images Europe. **p. 6** Axelle/Bauer-Griffin/FilmMagic/Getty Images. **p. 10** Gareth Cattermole/Getty Images Entertainment/Getty Images Europe. **p. 12** Mirek Towski/FilmMagic/Getty Images. **p. 26** Imago/Steve Vas/Alamy Stock Photo. **p. 31** Columbia Broadcasting System/Apatow Productions/Album/Alamy Stock Photo. **p. 33** Pictorial Press Ltd/Alamy Stock Photo. **p. 34** Photo 12/Alamy Stock Photo. **p. 35** (above) Entertainment Pictures/Alamy Stock Photo. **p. 35** (below) TCD/Prod.DB/Alamy Stock Photo. **p. 36** TCD/Prod.DB/Alamy Stock Photo. **p. 38** Collection Christophel/Alamy Stock Photo. **p. 39** Cinematic Collection/Alamy Stock Photo. **p. 41** (above) Entertainment Pictures/Alamy Stock Photo. **p. 41** (below) FOX Image Collection/Getty Images. **p. 42** FOX Image Collection/Getty Images. **p. 44** Pictorial Press Ltd/Alamy Stock Photo. **p. 45** RGR Collection/Alamy Stock Photo. **p. 47** Jeffrey Mayer/WireImage/Getty Images. **p. 48** Andreas Rentz/Getty Images Entertainment/Getty Images Europe. **p. 51** Entertainment Pictures/Alamy Stock Photo. **p. 5**2 Frederick Injimbert/ZUMA Wire/Alamy Live News/ZUMA Press, Inc./Alamy Stock Photo. **p. 54** TCD/Prod.DB/Alamy Stock Photo. **p. 55** Pictorial Press Ltd/Alamy Stock Photo. **p. 57** (above) Maximum Film/Alamy Stock Photo. **p. 57** (below) Cinematic Collection/Alamy Stock Photo. **p. 58** Foc Kan/WireImage/Getty Images. **p. 59** Dreamworks SKG/Cinematic Collection/Alamy Stock Photo. **p. 60** Niko Tavernice Film/Columbia Pictures/Cinematic Collection/Alamy Stock Photo. **p. 61** Columbia Pictures/Maximum Film/Alamy Stock Photo. **p. 62** Doug Peters/Alamy Stock Photo. **p. 65** Doug Peters/Alamy Stock Photo. **p. 66** Columbia Pictures/Album/Alamy Stock Photo. **p. 67** (above) Warner Bros/AJ Pics/Alamy Stock Photo. **p. 67** (below) TCD/Prod.DB/Alamy Stock Photo. **p. 69** Moviestore Collection Ltd/Alamy Stock Photo. **p. 70** Gravier Productions/Cinematic Collection/Alamy Stock Photo. **p. 71** Gravier Productions/AJ Pics/Alamy Stock Photo. **p. 72** Gravier Productions/Cinematic Collection/Alamy Stock Photo. **p. 73** (above) Pictorial Press Ltd/ Alamy Stock Photo. **p. 73** (below) Gravier Productions/Album/Alamy Stock Photo. p. 74 Fox Searchlight Pictures/AJ Pics/Alamy Stock Photo. **p. 75** 20th Century Fox/Photo 12/Alamy Stock Photo. **p. 76** Hoo-Me/SMG/Storms Media Group/Alamy Stock Photo. **p. 77** Elisabetta A. Villa/WireImage/Getty Images. **p. 80** Vittorio Zunino Celotto/Getty Images Entertainment/Getty Images Europe. **p. 82** Moviestore Collection Ltd/Alamy Stock Photo. **p. 83** Columbia Pictures/Cinematic Collection/Alamy Stock Photo. **p. 84** TCD/Prod.DB/Alamy Stock Photo. **p. 86** Black Label Media/Gilbert Films/Impostor Pictures/Marc Platt/Album/Alamy Stock Photo. **p. 88** David Crotty/Contributor/Patrick McMullan/Getty Images. **p. 90** Pictorial Press Ltd/Alamy Stock Photo. **p. 91** Collection Christophel/Alamy Stock Photo. **p. 92** Rune Hellestad/Corbis Entertainment/Getty Images. **p. 94** Element Pictures/Scarlet Films/Film4/Waypoint Entertainment/Album/Alamy Stock Photo. **p. 95** Twentieth Century Fox/Entertainment Pictures/ Entertainment Pictures/Alamy Stock Photo. **p. 97** (above) Columbia Pictures/Album/Alamy Stock Photo. **p. 97** (below) Jessica Miglio/Sony Pictures/Columbia Pictures/ Pariah/TCD/Prod.DB/Alamy Stock Photo. **p. 98** Twentieth Century Fox/Entertainment Pictures/Entertainment Pictures/Alamy Stock Photo. **p. 100** Kevin Winter/Staff/Getty Images Entertainment/Getty Images North America. **p. 101** Pictorial Press Ltd/Alamy Stock Photo. **p. 102** TCD/Prod.DB/Alamy Stock Photo. **p. 103** Walt Disney Pictures/Album/Alamy

Stock Photo. **p. 104** (above) Brad Barket/Stringer/Getty Images Entertainment/Getty Images North America. **p. 104** (below) Walter McBride/Contributor/WireImage/Getty Images. **p. 107** Walter McBride/Contributor/WireImage/Getty Images. **p. 108** Steve Granitz/ Contributor/ FilmMagic/Getty Images. **p. 110** Kevork Djansezian/Contributor/Getty Images Sport/Getty Images North America. **p. 112** Searchlight Pictures/Entertainment Pictures/ZUMAPRESS.com/ Alamy Sock Photo. **p. 114** Photo12/Searchlight Pictures/Alamy Stock Photo. **p. 115** Collection Christophel/Alamy Stock Photo. **p. 116** BFA/Atsushi Nishijima/Searchlight Pictures/Alamy Stock Photo. **p. 117** Kurt Krieger/Corbis/Contributor/Corbis Entertainment/Getty Images. **p. 118** Kevin Mazur/TCA 2011/ Contributor/WireImage/Getty Images. **p. 120** Alberto E. Rodriguez/Staff/Getty Images North America. **p. 122** Steve Granitz/Contributor/WireImage/ Getty Images. **p. 125** Jon Kopaloff/FilmMagic/Getty Images. **p. 129** Jeff Vespa/Contributor/ WireImage/Getty Images. **p. 130** Rodin Eckenroth/Stringer/Getty Images Entertainment/Getty Images North America/Getty Images. **p. 132** Vince Bucci/Stringer/Getty Images Entertainment/Getty Images North America. **p. 133** Kevin Winter/Staff/Getty Images Entertainment/ Getty Images North America. **p. 134** Kevin Winter/Staff/Getty Images Entertainment/Getty Images North America. **p. 137** Mike Coppola/Staff/Getty Images Entertainment/Getty Images North America. **p. 138** Searchlight Pictures/Entertainment Pictures/ZUMAPRESS.com/Entertainment Pictures / Alamy Stock Photo. **p. 140** Kevin Winter/Getty Images Entertainment/ Getty Images North America. **p. 141** Kevin Winter/Staff/Getty Images Entertainment/Getty Images North America. **p. 143** Jaguar/Alamy Stock Photo. **p. 144** Edward Berthelot/Contributor/Getty Images Entertainment/Getty Images Europe. **p. 146** David Crotty/Contributor/ Patrick McMullan/Getty Images. **p. 148** Dominique Charriau/Contributor/WireImage/Getty Images. **p. 149** Jeffrey Mayer/Contributor/WireImage/Getty Images. **p. 150** Daniele Venturelli/Contributor/WireImage/Getty Images. **p. 151** Neil Mockford/Contributor/FilmMagic/Gerty Images. **p. 153** (above left) Jeff Vespa/Contributor/WireImage/Getty Images. **p. 153** (above right) Steve Granitz/Contributor/WIreImage/Getty Images. **p. 153** (below) Cindy Ord/Staff/ WireImage/Getty Images. **p. 154** Jeff Kravitz/Contributor/FilmMagic/Getty Images. **p. 155** PA Images/Alamy Stock Photo. **p. 157** NDZ/Star Max/Contributor/GC Images/Getty Images. **p. 158** (above left) Frazer Harrison/Staff/Getty Images Entertainment/Getty Images North America. **p. 158** (above right) Edward Berthelot/Contributor/Getty Images Entertainment/ Getty Images Europe. **p. 158** (below) Andreas Rentz/Staff/Getty Images Entertainment/Getty Images Europe. **p. 159** Wiktor Szymanowicz/Future Publishing/Getty Images. **p. 161** Chris Polk/WWD/Penske Media/Getty Images. **p. 162** Marco Piovanotto/ABACAPRESS.COM/Abaca Press/Alamy Stock Photo. **p. 165** Retro AdArchives/Alamy Stock Photo. **p. 166** Jeff Vespa/ Contributor/Getty Images Entertainment/Getty Images North America. **p. 169** WENN Rights Ltd/Alamy Stock Photo. **p. 171** Shutterstock. **p. 173** Moviestore Collection Ltd/Alamy Stock Photo. **p. 176** Kate Green/Stringer/Getty Images Entertainment/Getty Images Europe. **p. 181** Vera Anderson/Contributor/WireImage/Getty Images. **p. 182** Samir Hussein/Contributor/ WireImage/Getty Images. **p. 184** Daniele Venturelli/Contributor/WireImage/Getty Images. **p. 187** Stephane Cardinale/Corbis/ Contributor/Corbis Entertainment/Getty Images. **p. 188** Twentieth Century Fox/Entertainment Pictures/ Alamy Stock Photo. **p. 195** Christopher Polk/ Staff/Getty Images Entertainment/Getty Images North America. **p. 196** Fred Duval/FilmMagic/Getty Images. **p. 202** Gareth Cattermole/Getty Images Entertainment/Getty Images Europe. **p. 204** Danny E. Martindale/Stringer/Getty Images Entertainment/Getty Images Europe. **p. 206–207** Taylor Hill/Contributor/FilmMagic/Getty Images.

PHOTO CREDITS 201

Acknowledgments

Whenever I see a book on the shelf, I think "How did that get made?!" There are so many people involved behind the scenes, making the writer look good. I want to thank the amazing team at Quarto who went above and beyond to help me to create an incredible book about a powerful role model. I learned so much from this project, not just from Emma/Emily Stone, who's positivity propels her success, but also from the publishing team: Rage Kindelsperger, Laura Drew, Cara Donaldson, Katie McGuire (wishing you the best!), Laura Klynstra, Shane Lowe, and Kot Copyediting & Proofreading.

Writing can be a lonely process, but even as I sit at my desk, there are hands on my back. Thanks to Laura Sebastian, Lauren H. Kerstein, Rhody Downey, Kathryn Otoshi, Ned Norman, and Jeff Waddleton, who all listened to me go on about how inspirational Emma is to me and sent me articles when Emma hit the news. Extra thanks to my wonderful agent, Deborah Warren. And to my husband, thanks for your ear and your gentle spirit—you encourage me at every opportunity and I am grateful.

Finally, the best advice I learned in the magical process of writing this book came from Emma herself: You're only human. You live once and life is wonderful, so eat the damn red velvet cupcake.

Thanks to all!

Stacia

Emma at the 62nd BFI London Film Festival, London, England, October 2018

About the Author

Stacia Deutsch is a *New York Times* bestseller, Scribe Award winner, and freelance author. With over twenty years of experience, Stacia has carved out her place in the pop-culture genre. She's written more than a dozen books linked to blockbuster films including *Batman: The Dark Knight* (2008) and *Ghostbusters* (2016), in addition to properties tied to popular television shows. Ghostwriting for a celebrity was on her bucket list, and now, Stacia can say she's done that three times! As a project editor, Stacia recently delved into the world of Barbie and all things pink. When she's not writing, Stacia can be found out on her ranch in Temecula, California, playing with dogs and horses, or at the movies researching her next book. Find her online at Instagram @ Staciadeutsch_writes , Facebook @staciadeutsch, or Bluesky: https://bsky.app/profile/staciawrites.bsky.social

Emma poses at the premiere of *Irrational Man* at the 68th Annual Cannes Film Festival in Cannes, France, May 2015

Following: Emma attends the 82nd Annual Golden Globe Awards in Beverly Hills, California, January 2025

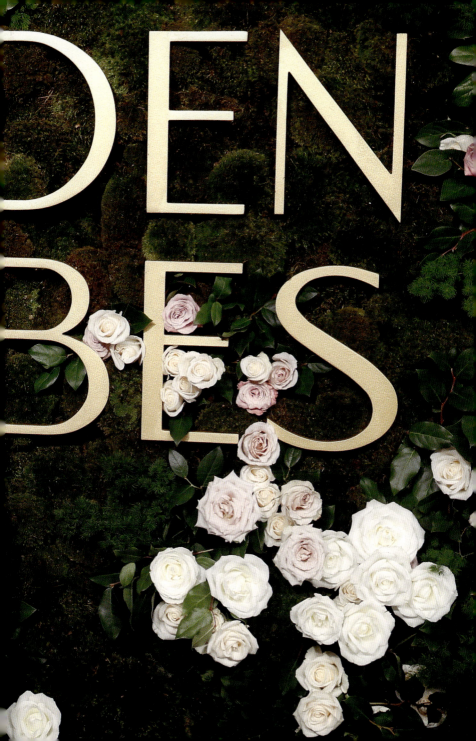

© 2025 by Quarto Publishing Group USA Inc.

First published in 2025 by Epic Ink, an imprint of The Quarto Group,
142 West 36th Street, 4th Floor, New York, NY 10018, USA
(212) 779-4972 • www.Quarto.com

All rights reserved. No part of this book may be reproduced in any form without written permission of the copyright owners. All images included in this book are original works created by the artist credited on the copyright page, not generated by artificial intelligence, and have been reproduced with the knowledge and prior consent of the artist. The producer, publisher, and printer accept no responsibility for any infringement of copyright or otherwise arising from the contents of this publication. Every effort has been made to ensure that credits accurately comply with information supplied. We apologize for any inaccuracies that may have occurred and will resolve inaccurate or missing information in a subsequent reprinting of the book.

Epic Ink titles are also available at discount for retail, wholesale, promotional, and bulk purchase. For details, contact the Special Sales Manager by email at specialsales@quarto. com or by mail at The Quarto Group, Attn: Special Sales Manager, 100 Cummings Center Suite 265D, Beverly, MA 01915 USA.

10 9 8 7 6 5 4 3 2 1

ISBN: 978-0-7603-9571-4

Digital edition published in 2025
eISBN: 978-0-7603-9572-1

Library of Congress Control Number: 2024951859

Group Publisher: Rage Kindelsperger
Creative Director: Laura Drew
Managing Editor: Cara Donaldson
Editors: Katie McGuire and Flannery Wiest
Cover and Interior Design: Laura Klynstra
Cover photo credit: Matteo Chinellato/NurPhoto/Getty Images

Printed in China

This publication has not been prepared, approved, or licensed by the author, producer, or owner of any motion picture, television program, book, game, blog, or other work referred to herein. This is not an official or licensed publication. We recognize further that some words, models' names, and designations mentioned herein are the property of the trademark holder. We use them for identification purposes only.